Perspectives of Gender and Language in Cameroonian Contexts

Edited by

Lilian Lem Atanga

Langaa Research & Publishing CIG
Mankon, Bamenda

Publisher:
Langaa RPCIG
Langaa Research & Publishing Common Initiative Group
P.O. Box 902 Mankon
Bamenda
North West Region
Cameroon
Langaagrp@gmail.com
www.langaa-rpcig.net

Distributed in and outside N. America by African Books Collective
orders@africanbookscollective.com
www.africanbookcollective.com

ISBN: 9956-791-75-X

© Lilian Lem Atanga 2013

DISCLAIMER
All views expressed in this publication are those of the author and do not necessarily reflect the views of Langaa RPCIG.

Bio-data of Authors

Dr Lilian Lem Atanga is a Senior Lecturer in gender and discourse studies in the University of Dschang, Cameroon. She has published among others a book on *Language, gender and power in the Cameroonian parliament in 2010* and *Gender and Language in African Sub-Saharan African Contexts: Tradition, Struggle and Change* with Ellece, Litosseliti and Sunderland.

Dr Jane Sunderland is a Senior Lecturer of Gender in Lancaster University, United Kingdom.

Dr Emmanuel Nforbi is a Senior Lecturer in the University of Dschang, Cameroon.

Dr Jean Romain Kouesso is a Senior Lecturer in the University of Dschang, Cameroon.

Professor Paul Mbangwana is the Registrar of the Cameroon Christian University, Bamenda.

Alice Tangang is a PhD Student at the University of Yaounde 1.

Caroline Ngamchara is an Assistant Lecturer in the Department of Sociology, University of Yaounde 1.

Raul Kasea is a Senior Lecturer in Ecole Normale Supérieur, University of Yaounde 1.

Caroline Stéphanie Jiogo Ngaufack is a Teaching and Research Assistant at the University of Dschang (Cameroon) in the area of translation.

Canisia Fontem is currently the pedagogic inspector for English Language in the West Region of Cameroon.

Akin Odebunmi is a Senior Lecturer in the Department of English, University of Ibadan, Nigeria.

Anna-Maija Pirttilä is a researcher in the University of Helsinki, Finland.

Table of Contents

Acknowledgements.. v

Section A: Theorising gender and language in Cameroon.... 1

1. Perspectives of Gender and Language in Cameroon............ 3
Lilian Lem Atanga

2. Language and Gender n African Contexts: Towards a Research Agenda... 11
Jane Sunderland

Section B: Gender and Literacy 19

3. Demasculinisation Des Centres d'alphabetisation : Le Cas Des Centres Du Programme National d'alphabetisation Dans La Menoua (Cameroun) 21
Jean Romain Kouesso

4. Gender and Literacy Practice in Africa: Case of Cameroon and Ghana 39
Emmanuel Nforbi

Section C: Representing Gender in Context 73

5. English Pedagogic Materials as Robust Vector of Gendering ...75
Paul Mbangwana and Alice Tangang

6. Genre et Langage dans L'espace Partisan Camerounais : La Promotion de la Femme Dans Les Productions Symboliques de L'UNC au RDPC 109
Caroline Ngamchara

7. Representation of Gender on Billboard and Poster Adverts of Brewery Products in Cameroon..123
Canisia Ndeloa, Lilian Lem Atanga, & Tsofack Jean Benoit

8. A Representation of Political Agents in Cameroon's Newspapers..141
Jiogo Ngaufack Caroline Stephanie

9. Taŋkáp System and Matrimonial Issues in Yemba Language......167
Raul Kassea

Section D: Gender in other contexts 176

10. How is the Acceptability of an Advertisement Determined?.....177
Anna-Maija Pirttilä-Backman & B. Raul Kassea[1]

11. Gender Representation in Religious Discourse in Nigeria....... 193
Akin Odebunmi

---

[1] English translation by Evelina Schmuckli; revised by Raul Kassea.

Acknowledgements

I would like to thank the following persons and institutions whose contribution to this volume cannot be underestimated.

My sincere gratitude goes to the University of Dschang for the financial support. This went a long way for the publication of this book.

Thanks also go to Dr Jane Sunderland for organising a seminar on gender and language in Cameroonian contexts, bringing together researchers interested in the area. This book is a result of the work of these researchers after the seminar.

Dr Roger Mondoue was the brain behind this project seeing the potential of working with Cameroonian researchers on gender and language to transform their reflections into scientific material.

Dr Sibonile Edith Ellece and Mr Alexandre Djimeli did a wonderful job in editing and commenting on the work. Indeed, their comments went a long way in bringing the work to its current state. I would also like to thank PROTOCOL for serving as a sounding board for my ideas.

Last but not least, I would like to thank my family and especially my mother, Esther and children, Jade Afunwi and Suh-Atanga for all the time I took away from them to prepare this work. Also to Honourine and Edwardine for being there.

To God be the Glory

Section A:
Theorising gender and language in Cameroon

1

Perspectives of Gender and Language in Cameroon

Lilian Lem Atanga
University of Dschang

There has been a paucity of gender studies in Cameroon compared to other fields in the social sciences. This has worse with studies relating to gender and language. The First department consecrated to gender related studies has been the Department of Women and Gender Studies in the University of Buea. Researchers in this department have published works most especially in the area of gender and development. Researchers including Endeley, Fonchingong, Fonjong and Fondo Sikod have been published. Although focusing on feminist studies, this department has paid little attention to both feminist linguistics and gender and language studies. Gender research has also been prevalent in other areas including medicine, agriculture, and psychology.

This does not however mean that there has been absolutely no literature in the area of gender and language. Researchers like Mbangwana (1996) have investigated naming patterns of married career women in Cameroon, especially high profile women. His investigation revealed that these women, as expected by traditional western culture (in contrast to traditional Cameroonian culture)[1] take the names of their husbands after marriage. The colonial legacy (though not institutionalised by law) required women to drop their maiden names after marriage. However, Mbangwana notes that these high profile career women, following an American tradition, in addition to their husband's names, retain their maiden names.

---

[1] By tradition, people from the Grassfield Bantu region (Northwest and West Provinces) have only one name which is their name, that is, their first name. They can only be referred to as' wife of X' but do not take the name of the husband. Only in the equatorial Bantu are girl-children referred to by the names of their fathers e.g. Ngo Nsom, where ngo means daughter of, and Nsom, the name of the father. So girl children and women do not have first names. Colonial practices made Cameroonian women take the names of their husbands, and children the names of their fathers.

Mbangwana argues that this is an expression of self affirmation. He gives examples such as: *Anne Nsang Nkwain* where the maiden name was Anne Nkwain, a name which used to be her 'public identity'. Taking up a new name, the husband's name – *Nsang*, prompts her to retain her maiden name *Nkwain* to preserve her old identity. Such a study points to the multiple identities (Wagner and Wodak 2006) of Cameroonian women both as traditional women who respect their culture and tradition and as modern, educated career women who want to assert their own personal success by maintaining their 'original' identities as children of their parents. After 2005 though, some MA and PhD thesis started focusing on aspects of gender and language. We have for example Atanga's 2007 PhD on the Cameroonian parliament and Tangang's 2009 PhD on gender and representation in English language textbooks in Cameroon. Gender and language is only beginning to gain mainstream attendance as it has been introduced as a course at the MA level in the Universities of Buea and Dschang in the Departments of English and Linguistics. This attention is beginning to yield fruits as some MA thesis are being done in the area including Ndeloa's 2009 on Gender representation in Brewery Adverts, Ameli Tabi's 2009 on Discursive construction of Gender in *100%Jeune* and Anu's discursive practices and its impact on female career choices. Some more students are currently researching within the area.

The paucity of research in gender and language does not signify the absence of researchable issues in gender and language. Gender ideologies in our society serve to perpetuate for example relations of dominance within our society. Vološinov (1973) and Thompson (1990: 8) indicate that ideologies are

> complex ways in which meaning is mobilised for the maintenance of relations of dominion ... This meaning is constructed and conveyed by symbolic forms of various kinds, from everyday linguistic utterances to complex images and texts.

Ideology and discourse are intricately linked since 'ideas' do not drift through the social world like clouds (Atanga 2010). Rather, ideas 'circulate in the social world as utterances, as expressions, as words which are spoken or inscribed' (Thompson 1984: 4).

The intention of this book is to bring out aspects of gender and language within the Cameroonian context looking at different domains of language study where gender is a variable.

Positioning Gender in contemporary Cameroon

As observed elsewhere, Cameroon is a fast changing nation and gender relations as well are changing with the times.

Situating Cameroon linguistically

Cameroon is a multi-ethnic, multicultural and multilingual country within the central African sub-region. It is an officially bilingual country with French and English as the official languages and over 250 national languages (see Ethnologue 2005). Being a country with such a complex linguistic profile and a multitude of ethnic groupings and cultures, there is then the difficulty of pointing to a 'Cameroonian' gender profile. Although there is this diversity of cultures and traditions, there is also a commonality in gender relations in Cameroon. Like most other African countries, these different ethnic groupings attach a lot of importance to culture and tradition.

Culture and tradition have a stronghold on gender relations in Cameroon. As Dahl (2006) observes, cultures can be very complex but a culture, large or small, can be broadly seen as 'shared' beliefs, values, customs, practices and normative 'rules' of social behaviour of a particular nation or people including ways of dressing, producing and also cooking food. These cultures, Dahl observes, are learned, shared, patterned, mutually constructed, symbolic, and arbitrary and internalised. These cultures tend to support gender differentiated roles and views them as beneficial.

Mostly, in a society with gender differentiated roles, men tend to do things differently from women. There are traditional structures that regulate relations between men and women. With colonisation and a collapse of some of these systems, traditional instruments which recognised gender differences but regulated these differences now fail to recognise gender equality, thus leading to abuse of women's rights.

The issue of women's rights and gender equality is abhorred in many Cameroonian societies as some men and women think that there cannot and should not be equality and equity between men and women as each of the sexes is distinct from the other, not only biologically but socially as in for example, 'women are cooks' (see Atanga 2009). This also holds true to the fact that men are seen as the heads of the family even when it is a woman who is responsible for the running of the family both financially and otherwise.

This sort of gender inequality between men and women in Cameroon has led to gender studies to be generally view as women's studies or feminist studies even when these are greatly different. A study of language to understand the representation of gender will be significant in the understanding of these relations.

The Collection

The chapters within this collection are basically descriptive with minimal qualitative analysis. As observed by Atanga et al (2012, 2013), this may actually be a good starting point as gender differences approach presents the perspectives of gender issues within the Cameroonian context and shows to what point discrimination within the Cameroonian society based on gender may actually be. Overt sexism as manifested in the parliament (Atanga 2007) and overt gender division of spaces (see Kuoesso this volume) are indicative of the fact that the Cameroonian society still has gender division of spaces and gender division of roles. Going with the trend in the field of gender and language which has moved from quantitative analysis yielding gender differences to qualitative analysis - the difference gender makes (see Mills 2002) may therefore be erroneous within the Cameroonian context. Although most of the papers are descriptive, some others such as Ndeloa et al, Jiogo and Ngamchara are analytical of gender and language use within institutional and cultural contexts. Most of the papers within the collection describe situations with gender inequalities.

This book therefore aims to examine current perspectives on gender and language in Cameroon contexts. The different chapters presented in the book below.

Organisation of the book

The book is organized into five sections grouping the chapters thematically. The first section, **Section A,** deals with the introduction and theoretical issues relating to gender and language in Cameroonian and African contexts. This section examines theories, methods and perspectives of gender and language in Cameroonian and African contexts. It examines the work done so far and the perspectives of this area of study within the African and especially the Cameroonian contexts. In this section, Atanga introduces the area of gender and language within the Cameroonian context and brings out the novelty of the area within this context. She presents the perspective of the kind of research being carried out in the area and the problems Cameroonian researchers encounter with researching gender and language. Sunderland gives an overview of gender and language studies within the African context and presents a research agenda. She indicates the gaps that need to be filled in research on gender and language in African contexts and theoretical and methodological issues.

Section B of the book examines gender and literacy in Cameroonian contexts. As indicated above, Cameroon has over 250 national languages and literacy in the official languages and national languages is being encouraged. The two papers in this section focus on both literacy in official languages (French and English), and literacy in the national languages. The papers examine the effects of gender relations in literacy practices in Cameroon. Kouesso examines the de-masculinisation of National Literacy Centres in the Menoua Division of the West Region of Cameroon. These literacy programmes are funded by the government for adult literacy in French, one of the official languages of Cameroon. The high attendance of these centres by women serves as a tool to keep away men from the centres, following the gender ideologies of the region that men and women do not share common space and do not compete or learn the same knowledge. These traditional gender ideologies, according to Kouesso, serve to keep men away from these literacy centres. Nforbi, on the other hand examines the role women play in literacy programmes. He notes that the elaboration of these programmes is not gender sensitive. Women are not involved in the elaboration of (national) literacy programmes and that although women constitute the majority of learners in most contexts, most of the teachers are men who usually are not sensitive to the needs of women.

Section C examines gender and linguistic representation in Cameroon. Unlike the other sections which are more quantitative, and base their findings more on differences in gender and language, this section is more qualitative. It examines language use in society. Mbangwana and Tangang examine language use in school textbooks of English and the stereotyping of gender roles. They examine traditional division of gender roles and identities recurrent in the school manuals which are replete with conservative traditional discourses, displaying women and girls as caretakers, cooks, baby-sitters, shoppers, lovers and many other inferior roles while those of men and boys are knowledgeable scientists, inventors, adventurers, providers of wealth and owners of things of high monetary value. Ngamchara looks at the discursive construction of women in political documents. She examines the CNU and CPDM constitutions of Cameroon to see how women are discursively constructed within these texts and how it affects women's participation in politics in Cameroon. It also shows the invisibility of women in Cameroonian politics.

Ndeloa examines the representation of gender in the advertisement of brewery products in Cameroon. She examines how women are discursively represented in billboard posters. These representations are generally gender biased presenting women in highly sexualized ways to be consumed by men. Ndeloa challenges this stereotyping of gender roles in adverts. Jiogo examines the representation of gender in newspapers in Cameroon taking the case of two newspapers. Her findings are indicative of the fact that the default gender in newspaper articles is masculine. She however finds out that there are emerging counter discourses that represent women as the leaders of tomorrow and the saviours of the African continent. Kasea explores the relationship between the language of marriage and the language of agriculture. Kasea argues that local linguistic and cultural practices are linked to the agriculture of the Yemba people and that some matrimonial arrangements were interpreted (especially) by foreign ethnologists to reify women as commodities, and these commodities were especially related to agricultural products. *Taŋkáp* was then translated as 'marriage lord' or literally 'father for money'.

Section D examines other papers from other African contexts other than Cameroon. These two papers from other African contexts are selected based on their generalisabily. The discussions within the papers in this section can easily be applicable to the Cameroonian context. Akin Obudenmi examines gender and representation in religious discourse in Nigeria. He examines language and gender use in theological contexts and notes that, even with the effort to deconstruct God in non-patriarchal terms, even female theologists, finding it difficult to deal with the situation. He does a micro analysis of language to come out with these difficulties of using gender neutral language within religious contexts. Anna-Maija Pirttilä-Backman And B. Raul Kassea expand a discussion on advertisement beyond the sphere of professionals in advertising and equality jurisprudence to include gendered and racial interpretations of people outside it.

2

Language and Gender in African Contexts: Towards A Research Agenda

Jane Sunderland
Lancaster University

This chapter does not report an empirical study, although it stresses the need for empirical studies. Rather, it looks at some issues raised when considering the topic of 'Language and Gender in African Contexts', and sketches out what might be included in a research programme.

First, and sadly, there is a large gap in the literature here. This is regrettable both for the study of African linguistics, and of language and gender itself (which is still very focussed on 'Western' contexts). Plenty can be found on the linguistics of African languages, including the functioning of *grammatical* gender (e.g. Katamba, 2006; Corbett, 2004; Corbett and Mtenje, 1987), and indeed on African sociolinguistics (e.g. Djite, 2008). There is also a huge amount of work on development and gender, for example the education of girls (see e.g. Ansell, 2002)[2], and literacy programmes in Africa for women. But the topic of gender and language in Africa (using *language* here in the sociolinguistic and discourse senses of 'language use'), though also very fruitful, is, to date, badly under-explored. Atanga et al 2012 and Atanga et a 2013 have greatly contributed to this field however.

This is not to say that Africa is a *particularly* 'special continent'. Every continent is surely 'special' in some way. And anything that happens in one continent varies hugely within that continent – both over space and over time. More importantly, anything that happens in one continent has 'echoes' outside it. As an example, in some communities in Botswana, young women are routinely given advice by older women prior to undergoing a traditional marriage; this takes place in a formalised, specific event (see e.g. Ellece, 2007). However,

---

[2] See also
http://www.theidlgroup.com/documents/girlseducationinAfrica.pdf

young people marrying in different 'Western' churches are also often similarly 'prepared' for marriage by a church leader. It is important to avoid even the suggestion of 'African essentialism'. Rather, something ('X') may be *characteristic* of a given African context – it is not a defining feature relevant to all its members, and is unlikely to be characteristic for ever.

What do we mean by 'African contexts'? Geographically, contexts extend from the entire continent through to a short-lived Community of Practice, taking in along the way the Sub-Saharan/North Africa distinction, nations, provinces and other regions, ethnic groupings (including those which cross national boundaries), towns, villages, transient events (such as markets and courts) – and would perhaps extend to the diaspora. In addition to geography, 'context' includes the historical and the socio-political, and such considerations need taking into consideration in the carrying out of research, analysis of data, and documentation associated with any piece of research.

How do we (even: can we) 'characterise' African contexts? To stick my neck out, a few suggestions are: cultures of orality, multi-lingualism/multi-ethnicity, respect for the elderly, strong family networks, gender differentiation, and sharp juxtapositions of the traditional and the modern – relative to some of the 'Western' world. These characteristics have implications for research topics, research questions and data. Below, at the risk of preaching to the converted, I give an indication of work already carried out in the area. My point is not so much to survey the field, as to highlight areas ripe for research.

Topics related to specific languages will vary with those languages. They include functions of the verb *marry* (and related lexis), the equivalent of which in Kinyarwanda (spoken in Rwanda) and Setswana and Ikalanga (spoken in Botswana) requires a male subject and female object, i.e. a man can 'marry' a woman, but not *vice versa* (Kimenyi, 1992). So 'Yohaáni yaróongoye Mariyá', i.e. 'John married Mary', can be said in Kinyarwanda, but not *'Mariyá yaróongoye Yohaáni'. We can posit an association between this and the marriage institution itself.

Sociolinguistic topics include the familiar ones of gender and language/dialect choice (considering questions of prestige and brokership), gender variation in tone (see e.g. Pearce (2009) on Kera in Chad), and alternative language styles (for example, the new use by young women of 'Student Pidgin' in Ghana (Dako, 2002; 2013)). Also of interest is *hlonipha*, a 'language of respect' characteristic of a dialect of Sesotho, which entails women being expected not to use certain lexis associated with sex, but instead 'baby language' equivalents. This does not serve them well when reporting sexual assault (Hanong Thetela, 2002). 'Taboo words' for women also exist in Kinyarwanda, in which a married woman cannot use the names of her parents-in-law or of some other relations, and even words which sound like these names (again see Kimenyi, 1992). There are likely to be unexplored similarities in other African languages and dialects.

In terms of discourse, *names* in many African languages are of interest because they are often lexically significant, and indeed gendered. Titles can also be important, in a particular gendered way. For example, married women academics in one Nigerian workplace tend to be known as 'Dr Mrs' (Mustapha, 2013.). African languages have their own terms of abuse for women (as do all languages) as well as gendered metaphors and proverbs; for the latter, how (and in what contexts) they are used are as of much interest as the proverbs themselves (see e.g. Yusuf, 1995, 1994). And, of course, there are (gendered) discourses surrounding a whole range of issues, for example, affirmative action (and the Beijing Declaration), sexual violence, domestic assault, HIV-AIDS, girls' schooling, domestic labour and childcare. There is also scope for the study of institutional discourse, e.g. in traditional and modern courts, schools, universities and parliament (see e.g. Atanga, 2009).

For Stylistics, topics include the representation of women and men in the language of modern and traditional songs, myths and folklore (as orature sites), and representations of gender in novels/plays by African writers, and of African women, men and gender relations by non-African writers. Stylistics need not stop at fiction, of course, and magazines and advertisements are other possible text-types which are almost always interesting in terms of gender representation.

There are various important issues for language and gender research here. One is feminism, which has underpinned much language and gender study, and indeed has been its driving force since the very early 1970s. However, in many African contexts, feminism has associations of being anti-family and anti-men. As everywhere, there are misunderstandings here, but these cannot be swept under the table. And there is now a journal called *Feminist Africa* .... It is important, I suggest, for anyone working on language and gender in an African context, to clarify that their work is not only 'about women', nor relevant only to women, but at the same time that the study of language and gender includes investigation of discursive structures of all sorts which, through intention or otherwise, promote discrimination against and disparagement of women in a range of fields.

A second issue is the theoretical approach underpinning a given piece of research. In the early stages of language and gender study in many 'Western' contexts, the dominant paradigm was 'gender difference', typically the way women and men spoke differently (often to each other) in a whole range of contexts. In many cases, similarities were found, and, in retrospect regrettably, these were often downplayed as being 'uninteresting'. Differences were also found (although it is more accurate to talk about 'differential tendencies', as it was rarely that case that all women talked in one way, all men in another). The question then was how to interpret these differential tendencies. Some researchers favoured the '(male) dominance' approach, i.e. they saw men speaking more than women, or interrupting more, or providing few 'minimal responses' in conversation, as a form of *linguistic dominance* of men over women. Other researchers (a little later, although the two approaches overlapped, and indeed still do) favoured a '(cultural) difference' approach, i.e. the idea that women and men are brought up in different 'linguistic sub-cultures', and hence have different conversational styles – which are nothing to do with dominance or power. (See Litosseliti, 2008, for a summary of these approaches.) What the two approaches had in common, however, was a focus on gender *differences*.

Most gender and language research nowadays does not look for such differences between women and men. There is an acknowledgement of gender similarities; more important is an appreciation of differential tendencies *among* women and *among* men; further, it is now also recognised that the way people talk varies hugely with the context, or Community of practice they are in. It will vary, inter alia, with their conversational goals, the people they are talking to (and others who may be listening), and their 'role' within that particular context or Community of practice. Another insight and which has led to developments in the field is that people have the tendency to 'perform' an identity through their talk; they don't just 'talk the way they do', in a very unconscious manner. This identity performance may include gender performance. A man or woman may speak in a certain way because they wish to be seen as a certain sort of man or woman – for example, sensitive, assertive or knowledgeable.

Rather differently, it is now recognised that people speak by 'drawing on' certain *discourses* which are available to them. Someone might, for example, articulate what we might call a 'gender equality' discourse (in a certain context); this as part of their 'identity performance'. Looking at discourses shifts the emphasis on language and gender study from the 'who' of talk (man, woman, girl, boy) to the 'what' (i.e. what is said in terms of ideas).

Of course, these newer ways of looking at gender and language are not only more intellectually sophisticated than the previous "(male) dominance' and '(cultural) difference' approaches, the focus of both of which was differential tendencies in the way women and men talk. However, the newer ways are also less about *disadvantage*. This is entirely appropriate in cultural contexts in which women are far *less* disadvantaged than previously – to the extent that sexism is described as 'subtle' (see e.g. Lazar, 2005; Mills, 2008) rather than overt. It is less appropriate in contexts in which the disadvantage of women and girls is not subtle at all. Researchers on language and gender in African contexts need to think carefully about which approach they are interested in adopting. There is no simple answer here. In some African contexts, women's and girls' disadvantage may not in fact be an issue at all (and any sexism very 'subtle' indeed). In other contexts, disadvantage may be glaring, and researchers working in such contexts will wish to look at linguistic dominance and its relationship to other social practices in which dominance is an issue.

Why am I, a UK citizen, resident in the UK, writing about language and gender in African contexts? Isn't this inappropriate, a form of neo-colonialism? I hope not. Non-Africans cannot and should not embark on such a project without being part of a wider network of African researchers (which I am). But surely non-Africans do have something to offer. One is the ethnographic 'outsider perspective' through which we can 'make strange' (and hence facilitate the exploration of) a little of what is familiar to our African colleagues (just as they can, for others, with non-African contexts). Secondly, much of

Africa, like everywhere else, is now distinctly 'global', and we are all a part of that.

References

Ansell, N. (2002) 'Secondary education reform in Lesotho and Zimbabwe and the needs of rural girls: pronouncements, policy and practice.' *Comparative Education* 38(1):91-112

Atanga, Lilian (2009) Gendered, Discourses and Power in the Cameroonian Parliament. Bamenda: Langaa Publishers

Atanga, Lilian (2007) Gendered Discourses in the Cameroonian Parliament. Unpublished PhD Thesis. Lancaster: Lancaster University.

Atanga, Lilian (2012) The Discursive Construction of a Model Cameroonian Woman in *Gender and Language*. 6/1

Atanga, Lilian (2013) *Gender and Language in SubSaharan Africa: Tradition, Struggle and Change*. Amsterdam: John Benjamins

Corbett, Greville (2004) *Gender*. Cambridge: Cambridge University Press.

Corbett, Greville and Mtenje, A. (1987) 'Gender agreement in Chichewa'. *Studies in African Linguistics* 18/1: 1 – 38.

Dako, Kari (2002) 'Student pidgin (SP) – the language of the educated male elite'. *IAS Research Review*, NS 18/2: 53 – 62.

Djite, Paulin (2008) *The Sociolinguistics of Development in Africa*. Multilingual Matters: Bristol, UK.

Ellece, Sibonile (2007) *The Discourse of Marriage Rituals in Botswana*. PhD thesis. Lancaster University, UK.

Hanong Thetela, Puleng (2002) 'Sex discourses and gender constructions in Southern Sotho: a case study of police interviews of rape/sexual assault victims'. *Southern African Linguistics and Applied Language Studies*. 20(3) 177-189.

Katamba, Francis (2006) 'Bantu nominal morphology'. In Derek Nurse and Gerard Philippson (eds.) *Bantu Languages*. Routledge: London, UK.

Kimenyi, Alexandre (1992) 'Why is it that women in Rwanda do not marry?' Paper presented at the *2nd Berkeley Women and Language*

Conference, Berkeley. See also http://www.kimenyi.com/language-women.php (accessed Dec. 2 2009)

Lazar, Michelle (2005) (ed.) *Feminist Critical Discourse Analysis: Gender, Power and Ideology*. London: Palgrave Macmillan.

Litosseliti, Lia (2006) *Gender and Language: Theory and Practice*. London: Hodder Arnold.

Mills, Sara (2008) *Language and Sexism*. Cambridge: Cambridge University Press.

Mustapha, Abolaji (2013) 'Variation in the address forms for Nigerian women in the workplace'.in Lilian Atanga, Sibonile edith Ellece, Lia Litosseliti and Jane Sunderland (eds.) *Gender and Language in SubSaharan Africa: Tradition, Struggle and Change*. Amsterdam: John Benjamins

Pearce, Mary (2009) 'Kera tone and voicing interaction'. *Lingua* 119: 846 – 864.

Yusuf, Yisa K. (1994) 'Proverbs and misogyny'. *Working Papers on Language, Gender and Sexism* 4 (2): 25-45.

Yusuf, Yisa K. (1995) 'Contradictory Yoruba proverbs about women. Their significance for social change'. In: Afonja, Simi and Aina, Bisi (eds.) *Nigerian Women in Social Change*. Ile-Ife: Obafemi Awolowo University Press. pp. 206-215.

Section B:
Gender and Literacy

Demasculinisation des Centres D'alphabetisation : Le Cas Des Centres du Programme National d'Alphabetisation dans la Menoua (Cameroun)

Jean-Romain Kouesso
Université de Dschang

Introduction

En dépit des actions multiformes d'éducation initiées depuis plusieurs décennies par les Etats, les organisations non gouvernementales et les institutions internationales, l'analphabétisme est toujours apparu comme un fléau planétaire affectant plusieurs centaines de millions d'enfants et d'adultes[3]. En l'an 2000, l'Institut de Statistique de l'UNESCO a estimé que le monde comptait près de 862 millions d'adultes analphabètes dont les 2/3, soit environ 575 millions, étaient des femmes (UNESCO 2004). De par le rôle prépondérant que ces femmes jouent au sein de la famille et de la société en général, la question de la promotion des programmes d'alphabétisation davantage centrés sur elles étaient ainsi devenue suffisamment préoccupante, de manière à revenir non seulement comme un sujet majeur de la littérature sur l'alphabétisation, mais aussi comme la priorité des programmes d'éducation des adultes (Chlebowska 1990, Horsman 1996 et UNESCO 2004). Aussi pourrait-on noter avec satisfaction l'important flux des femmes dans des centres d'alphabétisation comme ceux du Programme National d'Alphabétisation (PNA) dans le département de la Menoua au Cameroun. Mais comment comprendre le fait que ces centres d'alphabétisation se démasculinisent pendant qu'ils sont fortement sollicités par les femmes ? Pour tenter de trouver une réponse à cette interrogation, nous nous sommes appuyés sur une enquête sociolinguistique associant un questionnaire de description de centres d'alphabétisation, des interviews et une recherche

---

[3] Définition : *« Personnes âgées de 15 ans et plus »* (UNESCO 2004 : 6).

documentaire[4]. Le présent papier qui rapporte les résultats de l'enquête s'articule essentiellement autour de trois points : l'aperçu de l'alphabétisation dans le département de la Menoua, les manifestations et les facteurs de la démasculinisation des centres d'alphabétisation du PNA.

Aperçu de l'alphabétisation dans le département de la Menoua

Situation du département de la Menoua

Géographiquement, et de par les divisions administratives, le département de la Menoua se trouve dans la zone occidentale de la Région de l'Ouest Cameroun. Selon l'Institut National de la Statistique du Cameroun (2004), ce département s'étend sur une superficie de 1.380 km^2 et, en 2001, il comptait 372.244 habitants repartis dans 21 groupements et 3 agglomérations urbaines (Dschang le chef lieu du département, Penka-Michel et Santchou). Pour l'instant, il n'existerait pas une étude spécifique sur le taux d'alphabétisation des populations de la Menoua.

De par la diversité de son peuplement, la Menoua connaît une forte diversité linguistique. On y parle les deux langues officielles du Cameroun, le français et l'anglais, et quatre langues nationales. Pour la majeure partie de la population, le français est la première langue officielle et l'anglais la deuxième. Parmi les langues nationales, le yémba qui est la plus étendue couvre près de 2/3 du département. Les autres langues nationales sont : le mbo dans l'arrondissement de Santchou, le ngiemboon et le ghomala' dans l'arrondissement de Penka-Michel (Kouesso 2009).

Activités d'alphabétisation

Depuis la période précoloniale, le département de la Menoua a connu plusieurs modèles d'alphabétisation d'initiative privée ou publique.

---

[4] Cette enquête a été menée entre les mois de février et mai 2009. Elle a bénéficié d'une collaboration fort appréciable des encadreurs du PNA à qui je voudrais témoigner toute ma profonde gratitude. Je voudrais par ailleurs exprimer mes sincères remerciements à l'endroit du Dr Lem Lilian Atanga pour sa précieuse contribution à l'élaboration du présent article.

Les modèles d'alphabétisation d'initiative privée

Parmi ces modèles, on retrouve les initiatives du Chef Djoumessi Mathias, de la Société Internationale de Linguistique (SIL), du Cameroon Association for Bible Translation And Literacy (CABTAL), du Comité d'Etude de la Langue Yémba (CELY), du Comité de Langue Ngiemboon (CLN).

En s'inspirant de l'écriture bamoun, le chef Djoumessi Mathias de Foréké-Dschang entreprit en 1928 de développer l'écriture en langue yémba. Il s'en servira pour alphabétiser sa cour et former une équipe de sept alphabétiseurs au service de son groupement dans le cadre de l'Ecole de Langue Vernaculaire créée en 1931. Mais ouverte au public un an plus tard, cette école sera progressivement orientée vers l'éducation de la jeunesse pour devenir finalement une école publique classique (Momo 1997).

Depuis 1983, plusieurs membres de la SIL se sont installés dans le groupement Bafou pour le développement de la langue et la traduction des Saintes Ecritures (Starr 1989 et Momo 1997). C'est dans le cadre de ce projet que de nombreux jeunes et adultes de ce groupement et des groupements voisins, principalement Baleveng et Bamendou seront alphabétisées principalement en yémba. Dans le même sillage, le CABTAL a entrepris de créer depuis 1994 des centres d'alphabétisation dans le groupement Balessing où les populations s'initient à la lecture et à l'écriture du ngiemboom.

A la faveur du lancement en 1994 du projet Cameroon Mother Tongue Literacy, Education and Development par l'ANACLAC (Tadadjeu 2008), le CELY et le CLN ont créé dans leurs aires respectives plusieurs centres d'alphabétisation avec une option monolingue (langue maternelle) et une option bilingue (langue maternelle/langue française). Comme avec la SIL et le CABTAL, les modèles d'alphabétisation du CELY et du CLN s'inscrivent dans la logique de l'alphabétisation fonctionnelle. D'après Tirvassen (1997 : 26), celle-ci

> *Désigne l'enseignement qui consiste à transmettre, hors du contexte scolaire, des aptitudes de lecture, d'écriture et de calcul à des adolescents ou des adultes qui n'ont jamais été scolarisés ou qui, bien qu'il aient été à l'école, n'ont pas développé ces aptitudes suffisamment pour s'intégrer socialement et professionnellement dans leur communauté.*

Les apprenants y associent l'apprentissage de la lecture, de l'écriture et du calcul à la pratique des activités culturelles et socio-économiques au rang desquelles la lecture des textes bibliques, les chants, les danses, l'hygiène, la santé, l'alimentation, l'élevage, l'agriculture et l'apiculture.

Dans la mise en œuvre de ces modèles d'alphabétisation d'initiative privée, l'échelle numérique des apprenants dans une classe ne revêt pas une très grande importance pour leur fonctionnement. Aussi y trouve-t-on des centres d'alphabétisation de plusieurs dizaines d'apprenants, mais aussi de moins de dix. Il s'agit en l'occurrence soit des classes mixtes d'hommes et des femmes, soit des classes exclusivement d'hommes ou de femmes. Les effectifs d'apprenants des centres d'alphabétisation du CELY en 2001 et en 2002 (tableaux 1 et 2) et ceux de l'Antenne Balessing du CLN en 2001 (tableau 3) en sont une illustration.

Tableau 1 : centres d'alphabétisation du CELY en 2001

Centres d'alphabétisation	Niveaux	Total	Hommes	Femmes	Types d'apprenants
Asa' Wamba	I	03	01	02	Primo-analphabètes
	I	03	01	02	Semi-analphabètes
	I	11	05	06	Lettrés en français
	II	03	00	03	Semi-analphabètes
Asa'a Fonang	I	03	00	03	Semi-analphabètes
	II	02	00	02	Semi-analphabètes
Dschang	I	10	05	05	Lettrés en français
	III	01	01	00	Semi-analphabète
Penka-Michel	I	05	02	03	Lettrés en français
	II	07	01	06	Lettrés en français
Doumbouo	I	06	00	06	Semi-analphabètes
Bakoko	I+II	15	03	12	Semi-analphabètes
Mbeng	I	12	03	09	Semi-analphabètes
Baleveng	I+II	26	05	21	Semi-analphabètes
Ntsengbe	I+II	16	01	15	Semi-analphabètes
Fokoué	II	06	02	04	Semi-analphabètes
Total		129	30	99	

Source : CELY, Rapport synthétique d'activités du CELY 2000-2001, septembre 2001

Tableau 2 : centres d'alphabétisation du CELY en 2002

Centres d'alphabétisation	Niveaux	Total	Hommes	Femmes	Types d'apprenants
Penka-Michel A	I	32	15	17	Semi-analphabètes
Penka-Michel B	I	49	31	18	Semi-analphabètes
Ecole Publique de Folewi	I	8	3	5	Semi-analphabètes
Asaà' Wamba (Bafou)	I	6	2	4	Semi-analphabètes
Asaà' Fonang (Bafou)	IIA	5	2	3	Primo-analphabètes
	IIB	8	4	4	Semi-analphabètes
	I	15	4	11	Semi-analphabètes
Bamendou	I	2	1	1	Semi-analphabètes
Fokoué	II	3	0	3	Semi-analphabètes
Mezet	I	11	07	04	Lettrés en français
Total		139	69	70	

Source : CELY, Rapport annuel d'activités 2001-2002, octobre 2002

Tableau 3 : centres d'alphabétisation du CLN en 2001, Antenne de Balessing

Centres d'alphabétisation	Niveaux	Total	Hommes	Femmes
Bamewag	I	11	05	06
	II	06	02	04
Bambi	I	06	03	03
Balessing	I	12	09	03
Bametac	I	07	03	04
	II	11	08	03
Balessing Centre	I	09	05	04
Bawonwa	I	08	05	03
Collège la Dignité de Penka-Michel	I	64	28	36
Lycée de Penka-Michel	I	16	10	06
CAJA de Penka-Michel	I	12	07	05
Total		162	85	77

Source : CLN, Rapport et statistiques des classes d'alphabétisation 2000-2001, décembre 2000

Il ressort des tableaux 1, 2 et 3 que :

- les effectifs sont généralement assez réduits dans les centres d'alphabétisation des deux comités de langue. Les 27 centres d'alphabétisation concernés présentent en effet une moyenne de 16 apprenants inscrits par centre, soit 7 apprenants chez les hommes et 9 chez les femmes.

- dans les centres du CELY, les femmes sont les plus nombreuses alors que dans ceux du CLN, les hommes sont les plus représentés, même si on note certaines variations d'un centre à un autre ou d'une année à une autre. Cette tendance se reflète sur les autres données statistiques du CELY (1998 ; 1999 ; 2000) et du CLN, y compris les données sur le reste des centres d'alphabétisation de ce comité de langue situés dans le département du Bamboutos (CLN 2000 ; 2001).

Les modèles d'alphabétisation d'initiative publique

Nous en distinguerons principalement deux : la première Campagne Nationale d'Alphabétisation des années 60 et le Programme National d'Alphabétisation (PNA) de 2002.

A l'instar des autres départements du Cameroun, la Menoua a connu à l'aube des années 60 une vaste campagne d'alphabétisation de masse baptisée « Campagne Nationale d'Alphabétisation ». Dans les zones rurales où elle avait pour cible les paysans et les paysannes, cette Campagne était aussi connue sous l'appellation « Ecole sous l'arbre ». Plusieurs centres d'alphabétisation avaient fonctionné dans différents groupements du département de la Menoua. De nombreux adultes y avaient ainsi appris à la lire, à écrire et à compter en français, à l'instar de leurs enfants dans des écoles classiques. Selon un instructeur de l'Ecole sous l'arbre que nous avons rencontré, les apprenants étaient en très grande majorité constitués des femmes[5].

En septembre 2002, le Cameroun a lancé par le truchement du Ministère de la Jeunesse et des Sports (MINJES) son Programme National d'Alphabétisation. Inscrit dans la stratégie camerounaise de lutte contre la pauvreté, le PNA pour objectif général *« l'éradication progressive de l'illettrisme des populations du Cameroun, par la relance de l'alphabétisme fonctionnelle sur toute l'étendue du territoire national »* (MINJES 2002 : 11). A travers le PNA, le Cameroun cherche donc à résoudre les problèmes de développement auxquels fait cruellement face la frange analphabète de sa population en général, et de sa population féminine en particulier. Au lancement du PNA, ce pays comptait en effet près de 5 millions d'analphabètes dont 55 % de femmes. Ces propos du

---

[5] Nous n'avons malheureusement pas pu accéder aux statistiques des « Ecoles sous l'arbre » du département de la Menoua.

MINJES (2002 : 6) mettent d'ailleurs en exergue l'ampleur de l'analphabétisme féminin au Cameroun :

> *Si, pour l'ensemble de la population, l'analphabétisme est un fléau social et économique majeur, [...] ses effets sont encore plus néfastes quand il concerne la population féminine, en raison de la place et des rôles multiples que joue la femme dans la société.*

Dans le département la Menoua, les premiers centres du PNA appelés Centres d'Alphabétisation Fonctionnelle (CAF) ont été créés en mars 2005. Quatre ans après, nous y avons dénombré trente CAF fonctionnels où l'on apprend à lire, à écrire et à compter exclusivement en français, à l'exception d'un seul[6] dont la langue cible est l'anglais. Dans le présent article, nous ne nous intéresserons qu'aux 28 dont les encadreurs ont bien voulu répondre à notre questionnaire.

Manifestations de la démasculinisation des CAF

Dans les CAF, la démasculinisation se manifeste principalement par l'attrition du taux de masculinité des effectifs initiaux des centres d'alphabétisation et la faiblesse de la participation des hommes enregistrés comme des apprenants aux activités d'alphabétisation.

Attrition du taux de masculinité des CAF

Nous entendrons par taux de masculinité la proportion des hommes enregistrés par rapport à l'effectif total des apprenants. Notre appréciation de l'attrition du taux de masculinité des CAF dans le département de la Menoua prend comme point de départ les stratégies de mise en place de ces CAF et est basée principalement sur une comparaison entre leurs effectifs et ceux des comités de langues tableaux 1, 2 et 3.

Stratégies de mise place des CAF

Dans la mise en œuvre du PNA, les objectifs visés par le MINJES sont prioritairement quantitatifs : sortir de leur illettrisme un maximum d'analphabètes camerounais. C'est pourquoi appel a été fait aux

---

[6] Il s'agit du CAF de l'Ecole Publique G1 de Penka-Michel B.

stratégies de l'éducation de masse qui visent l'alphabétisation d'un plus grand nombre possible de personnes et présentent des avantages aux plans de l'accès, de la qualité et des coûts (MINJES 2002). Dans le cadre du déploiement de ces stratégies, l'ouverture d'un CAF est assujettie à l'enregistrement d'une moyenne de 30 apprenants. Généralement, les alphabétiseurs ou postulants au poste d'alphabétiseur procèdent par l'une des deux démarches suivantes:

Démarche n° 1 : convaincre les associations, les Groupes d'Initiatives Communes (GIC) et autres groupes rassemblant au moins 30 membres d'accepter l'alphabétisation comme l'une de leurs activités. Cette démarche permet de résoudre plus facilement le problème primordial des effectifs exigés.

Démarche n° 2 : mobiliser les membres de la communauté en vue de la création des regroupements au seul motif d'alphabétisation. Ici, l'alphabétiseur ou le postulant doit faire preuve de beaucoup de charisme et convaincre individuellement chaque potentiel apprenant.

Aussi les effectifs et la configuration des CAF recensés vont-ils refléter ces deux démarches.

Etat des effectifs dans les CAF

Dans le tableau 4 qui présente les effectifs d'apprenants des CAF dans la Menoua, nous avons scindé ces CAF en deux groupes : les CAF associatifs et les CAF non associatifs. Les premiers émanent de la démarche n° 1 et les seconds de la démarche n° 2 (tableau 4).

Tableau 4 : Centres d'Alphabétisation Fonctionnelle du département de la Menoua

N°s	Centres	Effectifs		
		Total	Hommes	Femmes
I. Centres d'Alphabétisation Fonctionnelle associatifs				
1	Azunla (Foréké-Dschang)	32	03	29
2	Balépé (Bafou)	43	10	33
3	Bamegwou (Fokoué)	30	15	15
4	Banza (Baleveng)	54	01	53
5	Bassessa (Bafou)	32	00	32
6	Commune de Fongo-Tongo	36	04	32
7	Ecole Publique Meket (Fondonera)	40	02	38
8	Fotsem Lessing (Foréké-Dschang)	36	04	32

9	GIC de Nsui (Foto)	30	00	30
10	GIC PROMEAC (Foto)	31	19	12
11	Keagni (Baleveng)	35	01	34
12	Kemgwa'a (Foto)	35	12	23
13	Mossa letsi kemjio (Baleveng)	30	04	26
14	Poomezong Lekouet (Bamendou)	34	02	32
15	Santchou 1	24	06	18
16	Tchouaffi (Foréké-Dschang)	32	04	28
17	Tsintsué (Foréké-Dschang)	31	03	28
	Total I	**585**	**88**	**495**
	II. Centres d'Alphabétisation Fonctionnelle non associatifs			
1	Baleveng Centre	52	01	51
2	Balevoni (Foto)	30	05	25
3	Collège Privé Bilingue Santchou	32	01	31
4	Commune de Nkonzem	33	00	33
5	Ecole Publique de Fomopéa	26	00	26
6	Ecole Publique G1 de Penka-Michel A	32	07	25
7	Ecole Publique G1 de Penka-Michel B	33	03	30
8	Fontsa-Toula	32	06	26
9	Quartier Haoussa (Dschang)	32	10	22
10	Saakia (Bafou)	31	04	27
11	Tsobing (Baleveng)	35	01	34
	Total II	**368**	**38**	**330**
	Total I + Total II	**953**	**128**	**825**

Le tableau 4 révèle que les 28 CAF associatifs et non associatifs sont fréquentés par 953 apprenants, à raison de 128 hommes et 825 femmes. Les hommes y représentent ainsi 13,43 % d'apprenants, et les femmes 86,56 %. A l'exclusion du GIC PROMEAC où l'on retrouve plus d'hommes (19) que de femmes (12) pour un total de 31 apprenants, et du centre d'alphabétisation de Bamegwou où les 30 apprenants sont répartis équitablement en 15 hommes et 15 femmes, tous les autres CAF ont des effectifs soit exclusivement féminins, soit mixtes, mais à une très faible représentation masculine. La moyenne générale des inscrits par CAF est ainsi de 34 apprenants, à raison de 05 apprenants chez les hommes et 29 chez les femmes. Par rapport aux centres d'alphabétisation du CLN et du CELY (tableaux 1, 2 et 3), cette moyenne des inscrits par centre dans les CAF a connu une nette augmentation.

Seulement, à regarder de près, l'augmentation des effectifs affichée par le tableau 4 concerne uniquement les femmes. Chez les hommes, on constate non pas une augmentation, mais plutôt une diminution des effectifs. Ainsi, pendant que l'effectif des femmes s'est plus que triplé, celui des hommes a plutôt subi une diminution de près d'un tiers. Ceci constitue un indicateur par excellence de la démasculinisation des CAF.

Par ailleurs, une comparaison de la présence masculine dans les CAF associatifs et dans les CAF non associatifs du tableau 4 nous permet de noter que dans les premiers, la moyenne des inscriptions masculines est de 5 apprenants alors que dans les seconds elle est de 4. En effet, si les hommes sont plus nombreux dans les CAF associatifs, c'est parce qu'ils étaient au départ inscrits comme des membres d'une association, d'un GIC ou autre regroupement avant d'être contraints par solidarité de se convertir en apprenants. Dans ces conditions, il n'est pas aisé d'apprécier le degré de conviction des uns et des autres par rapport aux activités d'alphabétisation. Dès lors, nous pensons que les repères les plus indiqués d'appréciation des effectifs masculins dans les centres d'alphabétisation du PNA devraient être les CAF non associatifs qui affichent par centre une moyenne de 4 hommes.

Il ressort de ce qui précède que malgré l'absence d'une politique spécifique d'alphabétisation des femmes, les stratégies d'éducation de masse adoptée par le PNA conduisent à une nette augmentation du nombre de femmes dans les centres d'alphabétisation. Mais en revanche, il s'en une diminution non négligeable des effectifs d'hommes. Nous reviendrons sur les principaux facteurs des cette diminution (cf. § 4).

Faible participation des hommes aux activités d'alphabétisation

La participation des hommes enregistrés comme des apprenants aux activités dans les CAF est fonction de leurs attitudes et comportements vis-à-vis de l'alphabétisation. Nous ne nous intéresserons ici qu'aux types de comportements qui contribuent à l'érosion de la présence masculine dans les CAF. Certains de ces comportements sont spécifiques à la configuration associative ou non associative des CAF alors que d'autres leur sont communs.

S'agissant des comportements spécifiques à la configuration des CAF, nous noterons que :

- dans les CAF associatifs, les hommes se montrent très actifs pendant les activités initiales des groupes. Mais lorsque vient l'heure des activités d'alphabétisation, ils sont généralement portés disparus.

Les plus polis d'entre eux s'excusent en ces termes : « *continuez, on arrive* », « *je prends juste quelque chose à côté* », etc. A travers ce type de comportement, on peut déceler le peu d'intérêt que ces hommes accordent à d'alphabétisation, comparativement aux activités initiales de leurs associations ou à certaines autres activités qu'ils jugent plus utiles ou plus commodes.

- dans les CAF non associatifs, les hommes assistent généralement aux cours dans les débuts. Mais quelque temps après, ils accusent de nombreuses absences. Cet absentéisme, faut-il le souligner, n'est pas caractéristique des hommes seuls. D'après un responsable du PNA, il fait partie du quotidien de centres d'alphabétisation non associatifs : « *Au début, les populations viennent nombreuses. Mais avec le temps, elles peuvent se désintéresser. Généralement après six à douze mois de cours, le taux global de fréquentation se situe entre 40 et 50 % dans les groupes non organisés* ».

Parmi les comportements communs aux CAF associatifs et CAF non associatifs, on relève les discours visant à décourager les apprenants et le refus des hommes d'arborer l'uniforme de la Journée Internationale de l'Alphabétisation.

Les discours visant à décourager les apprenants. Ces discours sont généralement tenus par les hommes même s'ils sont souvent aussi entendus de la bouche des femmes. En voici quelques uns qui ont été repris par certains des apprenants que nous avons rencontrés :

- « *Si tu n'as pas réussi avec l'école, ce n'est pas l'alphabétisation qui fera de toi quelque chose* » ;
- « *Depuis qu'on dit que l'alphabétisation va changer ma vie, je ne vois rien* » ;
- « *Les enfants ne font rien avec l'école, c'est nous qui allons faire quoi avec ?* » ;
- « *L'école c'est pour les enfants et non pour les vieux* ».

Le refus d'arborer l'uniforme de célébration de la Journée Internationale de l'Alphabétisation : à l'occasion de cette journée, les apprenants et les sympathisants portent habituellement une tenue de circonstance. Mais de nombreux témoignages révèlent que les hommes sont généralement sceptiques au port de cette tenue. Pendant les dernières célébrations de la Journée Internationale de l'Alphabétisation, il est ainsi apparu que les hommes confectionnaient des uniformes, non pas pour eux-mêmes, mais plutôt pour leurs épouses.

Le résultat de ces comportements est que des hommes inscrits dans les CAF, ceux qui participent encore aux activités d'alphabétisation sont très réduits. Voici pour l'illustrer quelques données rapportées par les alphabétiseurs :

- CAF de Bamegwou (associatif ; 15 hommes sont inscrits) : seuls 05 hommes en moyenne prennent régulièrement part aux activités ;
- CAF de Kemgwa'a (associatif ; 12 hommes inscrits) : « *Les hommes ne prennent pas part aux activités d'alphabétisation. Depuis il y en a eu deux qui sont aussitôt repartis* » ;
- CAF de Baleveng Centre (non associatif, 01 homme inscrit) : l'unique homme inscrit a pris part à 10 séances de cours sur les 12 ;
- CAF du quartier Haoussa (non associatif ; 10 hommes inscrits) : 05 hommes en moyenne prennent régulièrement part au cours ;
- CAF de l'Ecole Publique de G1 de Penka-Michel A (non associatif ; 07 hommes inscrits) : 02 hommes en moyenne sont réguliers aux cours.

Au bout du compte, la participation des hommes aux activités d'alphabétisation dans les CAF se situe en deçà des attentes correliées aux taux de masculinité des effectifs.

Facteurs de la démasculinisation des CAF

La démasculinisation des CAF apparaît comme le résultat de la conjonction et de l'interaction de trois facteurs qui ont un rapport plus ou moins direct avec la mise en œuvre du PNA : la violation de l'hégémonie masculine, l'environnement psycho-social et certaines faiblesses du programme d'alphabétisation.

Violation de l'hégémonie masculine

L'expression de domination des femmes au niveau des centres d'alphabétisation apparaît comme une violation d'une hégémonie masculine habituellement caractéristique des rapports entre l'homme et la femme. La masculinité hégémonique ou domination masculine consacre en effet une suprématie physique ou symbolique de l'homme. Loin d'être une donnée naturelle, elle émane d'une construction culturelle et sociale « naturalisée », incorporée dans les schémas de pensée des individus et traduites dans les discours, les comportements, les pratiques sociales (Connell 1995 ; Bourdieu 1998 ; Eckert et Ginet 2003, Connell et Messerschmidt 2005). Dans le département de la Menoua, les indicateurs de la masculinité hégémonique peuvent se décliner en termes de puissance, de conquête, de domination, de prestige, de famille polygame et de société patriarcale alors ceux de la féminité généralement dominée se déclinent pour l'essentiel en termes de faiblesse, douceur, de soumission et d'objet de conquête. Chez les adultes et les autres personnes âgées, il est par exemple observable qu'en route les hommes marchent devant et les femmes (et les enfants) derrière eux, que le côté droit chez l'espèce humaine représente la famille paternelle, et le côté gauche la famille maternelle. En établissant une infériorisation ou une incapacitation de la femme, certains proverbes comme *« Les urines d'une femme ne traverse pas un sillon »* ou *« Qu'est-ce tu peux entendre de la bouche d'une femme ? »* participent également des stratégies de la construction de la masculinité hégémonique.

L'on peut ainsi comprendre que l'affluence massive des femmes dans les centres d'alphabétisation depuis l'Ecole sous l'arbre ait créé une impression populaire et péjorative selon laquelle l'alphabétisation n'était que « l'école des femmes ». Il n'est donc pas rare d'entendre les hommes s'interroger en ces termes : *« Akóö azi o a juñó laö ? Meñ ndókó asikuàu ewónzwüü meà eàgóö ? »* (*Que dis-tu là ? Je vais où avec l'école des femmes ?*). Aux yeux des hommes, l'alphabétisation ne revêt aucune importance et ne confère aucune autorité. C'est alors que pour eux, fréquenter un centre d'alphabétisation revient à se manquer du respect. Comme l'affirme un alphabétiseur, *« Les hommes ont honte de laisser transparaître leur analphabétisme. Il y va de leur autorité d'homme. Il est hors de question qu'on les voit en train d'apprendre à écrire ou à lire »*. Au lieu d'exposer leur incompétence à lire et à écrire devant les femmes, les hommes préfèrent donc l'étouffer en donnant généralement l'impression qu'ils sont très occupés.

Environnement psycho-social

Comme dans bien de localités du Cameroun, les populations du département de la Menoua ont connu ces dernières années de nombreux projets de lutte contre la pauvreté initiés par les comités locaux de développement, les organismes non gouvernementaux ou l'Etat. Dans la plupart du temps, ces projets se sont matérialisés par la réalisation des œuvres sociales telles que la construction des points d'eau, des routes et autres infrastructures sociales. Ils se sont aussi manifestés par un appui matériel ou financier aux organisations spécialisées dans les activités commerciales, artisanales, piscicoles, agricoles et pastorales. De par les actions ainsi menées à leur faveur, les populations ont fini par retenir que telle était l'approche standard de la lutte contre la pauvreté. Et lorsque l'alphabétisation leur est présentée fonctionnelle comme un outil de développement et de lutte contre la pauvreté (MINJES 2002 ; Mekon 2005), elles s'attendent à bénéficier des avantages similaires à ceux auxquels elles étaient habituées. C'est ce qui a d'ailleurs poussé certains hommes à s'engager dans l'alphabétisation. Mais quand ils se rendent compte que la réalité est toute autre, ils n'hésitent pas à se retirer.

Parlant de la désertion des hommes de son CAF, un alphabétiseur affirme :

> *Quand les hommes inscrits dans mon centre acceptaient de s'alphabétiser, ils croyaient surtout que l'association allait bénéficier d'une aide matérielle ou financière du PNA. Mais quand ils ont réalisé plus tard que ce n'était pas ça, ils ont estimé qu'ils perdaient leur temps. Ils n'assistent plus aux cours...Il faut comprendre qu'un homme ne sort pas de chez lui pour rien. Tout ce qu'il fait doit lui rapporter quelque chose.*

Il en ressort que de par sa stratégie de lutter contre la pauvreté, les CAF n'ont pas comblé les horizons d'attente de beaucoup d'hommes.

Faiblesses du programme d'alphabétisation

Deux faiblesses du programme contribuent à inhiber la présence des hommes dans les centres d'alphabétisation. Il s'agit de l'insuffisance des solutions apportées aux besoins des apprenants et la configuration des classes.

- L'insuffisance des solutions apportées aux besoins des apprenants. Comme motif de leur désertion des cours d'alphabétisation, certains hommes évoquent la non satisfaction de leurs besoins. L'un deux déclare en effet :

Au début, il n'y avait pas de problème. Nos doléances avaient été posées, mais n'ont pas trouvé de solution… Il n'y a pas d'activités pratiques comme nous souhaitons. Nous sommes des adultes, et des adultes responsables. Le a, b, c va nous apporter quoi ? » …L'élevage des porcs ou des poulets, la fabrication du compost, la culture des pommes de terre sont par exemple nécessaires pour lutter contre la pauvreté.

Pour ces hommes, tout comme pour l'ensemble des apprenants, les activités pratiques constituent la seule raison d'être d'un centre d'alphabétisation.

- La configuration des centres d'alphabétisation. Dans chaque centre d'alphabétisation du PNA, tous les apprenants sont regroupés dans une classe unique indépendamment de leur sexe, de leur degré d'analphabétisme ou de leur référence sociale. Un tel cadre est de nature à frustrer et décourager certaines personnes, et principalement les hommes. Selon certains alphabétiseurs, les hommes n'acceptent pas de se retrouver dans un même endroit que leurs épouses, leurs enfants ou leurs belles-mères, tout comme les nantis n'aimeraient pas apprendre dans les mêmes conditions que les démunis. De nombreux hommes parmi les opérateurs économiques, les hommes politiques et autres dont le niveau de scolarisation ne leur permet pas d'être suffisamment opérationnels dans leurs secteurs d'activités aimeraient bien s'alphabétiser, non pas dans des centres populaires que sont les CAF, mais dans des cadres socialement homogènes et présentant des effectifs plus restreints.

Conclusion

Tout en nous réjouissant de ce que les femmes du département de la Menoua sont massivement représentées dans les centres d'alphabétisation du PNA, nous avons voulu examiner les manifestations et les facteurs de la démasculinisation que connaissent par ailleurs ces centres. Parmi les manifestations, nous avons relevé l'attrition d'effectif des apprenants masculins et la faible participation de ces derniers aux activités d'alphabétisation. Au rang des facteurs de la démasculinisation des centres d'alphabétisation, nous nous sommes appesanti sur la violation de l'hégémonie masculine, l'environnement psycho-social et deux faiblesses du programme d'alphabétisation que sont l'insuffisance des solutions apportées aux besoins des apprenants et la configuration des centres d'alphabétisation. Tout ceci nous permet d'attirer l'attention des acteurs de l'alphabétisation sur le fait que dans la Menoua et sans doute ailleurs, les hommes pourront bientôt rejeter et déserter totalement les centres d'alphabétisation. Pour prévenir une telle situation, nous plaidons pour que les hommes soient comme retenus une cible spécifique de la sensibilisation et l'information sur l'alphabétisation. Nous plaidons aussi pour que des efforts soient davantage consentis en vue, d'une part, de garantir l'effectivité de la fonctionnalité des centres d'alphabétisation et, d'autre part, de restructurer ces centres en tenant compte des besoins globaux et spécifiques des apprenants. Dans cette optique, les résultats quantitatifs cesseront d'être considérés comme l'objectif primordial de l'alphabétisation afin de permettre l'agrément des centres qui auraient moins de trente apprenants.

Références bibliographiques

Bourdieu, P. (1998) *La domination masculine*, Paris : Seuil.
Chlebowska, K. (1991) « Les femmes rurales africaines », in *Diagonales*, EDICEF, Paris N° 17, [32-33].
CELY. (2001) *Rapport synthétique d'activités du CELY 2000-2001*, septembre 2001.
CELY. (2002) *Rapport annuel d'activités 2001-2002*, octobre 2002.
CLN. (2000) *Rapport et statistiques des classes d'alphabétisation 2000-2001*, décembre 2000.
Connell, R.W. (1995) *Masculinities*, Berkeley and Los Angeles : The University of California Press.
Connell, R.W. et Messerschmidt, J.W. (2005) « Hegemonic masculinity : rethinking the concept »,
http://history.anu.edu.au/files/documents/Connell&Mess_HegemonicMasc.pdf (consulté le 04 mai 2009).
Eckert, P et Ginet, S.M. (2003) *Gender and language*, Cambridge : Cambridge University Press.
Horsman, J. (1996) « Literacy and gender »,
http://www.jennyhorsman.com/articles/gender/ymca.pdf (consulté le 16 avril 2009).

Institut National de la Statistique (Cameroun). (2004) *Annuaire statistique du Cameroun*, Yaoundé : Institut National de la Statistique.

Kouesso, J. R. 2009. *Variation dialectale et standardisation de l'orthographe du yémba*. Thèse de Doctorat/PhD, Yaoundé : Université de Yaoundé I.

Mekon, P. (2005) « L'alphabétisation fonctionnelle : un outil de développement local et de lutte contre la pauvreté », communication présentée au Séminaire atelier national de formation des chefs de pôles et des superviseurs départementaux aux nouvelles méthodes didactiques d'alphabétisation fonctionnelle du 05 au 07 octobre 2005 à Bafoussam.

MINJES. (2002) *Programme National d'Alphabétisation,* Yaoundé : Ministère de la Jeunesse et des Sports

Momo, G. (1997) *Le yémba : histoire de la langue écrite dans la Menoua*, Dschang : CELY.

Tirvassen, R. (1997) « Alphabétisation fonctionnelle », in Moreau, M. L. (éd) *Sociolinguistique : les concepts de base*, Bruxelles : Mardaga.

Starr, A. (1989) « Sociolinguistic survey of Yemba and Ngyemboon Eastern Grassfield languages of Cameroon » Yaoundé : SIL.

Tadadjeu, M. (2008) « Enhancing the role of African languages in local development projects », in Mutaka, N.M. (ed) *Building capacity : using TEFL and African languages as development-oriented tools*, Langaa Resarch and Publishing CIG : Bamenda.

UNESCO. (2004) *La décennie pour l'alphabétisation : ses débuts 2003-2004*, Paris : UNESCO.

4

Gender and Literacy Practice in Africa: Case of Cameroon and Ghana

Emmanuel Nforbi,
University of Dschang

UNESCO (2008) indicates that there are 774 million adult illiterates in the world making about 1/5 of the world's population; nearly 2/3 is women. 124, 718, 600 (16.1%) of the 774 million world illiterates adults are found in sub Saharan Africa; 57 percent being women. There are 22 countries of the world that more than ½ of their population is illiterate 15 of them are in Africa.

The two African countries studied here have the following UNESCO (2002) projections for 2010 literacy rates: 82% for Cameroon and 82.6% for Ghana. The gender statistics indicate 13.3% for the males and 23.1% for females in Cameroon and 12.5% for male in Ghana against 24.2% for females for the same year.

Out of the 181 million illiterates in Africa, 112 million are women and 69 million are men. In terms of overall population and illiterate rates in Africa, the women pose a serious threat.

Table 1: Illiterates in sub-Saharan Africa, 15 years and above: projections for 2010

	15 to 24 years	25 to 64 years	65 + years	Total	
Male	17.796.870	31.128.320	4.484.230	53.409.420	42.82%
Female	17.514.300	43.874.430	7.920.490	71.309.220	57.17%
Total	35.311.170	77.002.430	12.404.680	124.718.600	

Table 2: Summary of literacy rates in Africa, Cameroon and Ghana: UNESCO (2002) projections for 2010

	Africa	Cameroon	Ghana
Overall	69.2%	82%	82.2%
Male	76.5%	87%	87.5%
Female	63.1%	77%	75.8%

From the above table, we realize that the two countries are at the level of the World literacy rate and above the overall literacy rate for Africa. This is an indication that these two countries are seriously involved in the fight against illiteracy in the continent. Looking at the figures of female literacy, we observe that these two countries still need to do something about their female literacy rates. An evaluation of their activities from a gender perspective will therefore give us a clearer picture of literacy and gender in Africa.

The gender problem in Africa is clearly evident in the practice of literacy. Even though the illiteracy situation shows two thirds of the world's illiterates as women, they have not been empowered to face this challenge. In this paper, there are indicators to demonstrate that women are marginalized. It would be ideal that those managing literacy activities as well as the instructors should be two-thirds women and not the contrary. The data for this study has been collected both ethnographically and through documentary surveillance of literature and archives relating to literacy in Cameroon and Ghana.

Gender and Literacy in Cameroon

After the collapse of the government run adult literacy programme in the sixties, efforts in both mother-tongue literacy and official language (English and French) literacy have been revived within the last twenty years in Cameroon. The summer institute of linguistics (SIL), the Cameroon Association for Bible Translation and Literacy (CABTAL), and the National Association of Cameroonian Language Committees (NACALCO) have been at the forefront of mother-tongue literacy in Cameroon.

The SIL literacy programme has been run mostly by women actively involved in conceiving and implementing these programmes.

On the contrary, the NACALCO programmes have been essentially run by men. The President of NACALCO and his important collaborators have been men. Less than 5 % of women have been in the bureau of NACALCO for the past 20 years. NACALCO successfully enabled the creation of over 100 language committees and trained hundreds of literacy instructors and thousands of learners in Cameroon. Out of the over one hundred language committees representing different Cameroonian languages, none of the presidents has been a woman. The women filled the classrooms as learners and pre-literates. In literacy instructors training courses, the contrary has been true.

Case Studies

Women In Literacy And Development In Cameroon
The situation within the last twenty years shows that women are not playing leading roles in literacy. In January 1996 at a literacy instructors training course, organized by SIL, in Maroua, out of the over 30 participants, there was no female participant. After enquiries, it was discovered that the men left their wives behind because it was not the tradition for the women to leave their homes and stay out for two weeks. One of the participants then asked the following question to the researcher:

"Who will take care of the children, prepare food for them and take care of the house?"

A similar course organized in the North-West Region of Cameroon, registered 35 participants and only 3 were women making a total of 8%. The response of the men was not very different from that of the men in the Far North. The women needed to take care of the family in their absence.

It should be noted that in the Far North Region, an essentially Muslim region, about 90% of the girls get married before the age of twenty and as much as this percentage do not complete primary education if at all they start it. It can be estimated that in the primary schools, over 80% are boys.

Traditionally, the women have come to believe that marriages and home making is their vocation. This assumption has not always been true due to the harsh economic situation in Africa. Women have come to shoulder much of the responsibility of the family economically and social wise. Women therefore need more than ever before education that will fit them into a profession. The fulfilment of this responsibility through the provision of special educational facilities for adult women is nothing more than paying an old debt that has been long overdue and it should not therefore be regarded as favour to them.

The state of the world population (1990) reported that the results of studies carried out in 46 countries indicated that a 1% increase in women's literacy rate is three times more effective in reducing infant mortality than a 10% increase in the number of doctors. As women's level of education rises, the number of malnourished children declines. According to recent UNICEF sources (2002), educating girls for six years or more drastically improves their prenatal care, postnatal care and childbirth survival rates.

Unfortunately, there are difficulties involved in employing mature women because of lack of necessary educational qualification. There is therefore need for re-schooling to prepare them for a place in the working world.

This problem of reschooling was faced by women groups in Cameroon like the Women's Department of the Federation of Protestant Churches (FEMEC) and other women's non-governmental organizations like the Association of Women Information Co-Ordination Office (AWICO). Through the integration of literacy programmes in their schemes, functional literacy can be attained.

Women's Involvement in Literacy

Through non-governmental organizations involved in helping women to develop themselves through self-help activities, most preliterate women are now seeing the need for literacy and are asking for it. In 1997 a women's group based in Balikumbat, Ngoketunja Division, North West Region of Cameroon did express the need to learn how to read and write. They strongly expressed this desire because they realized that they could not manage their activities by themselves. They ran a corn mill and could record the income and expenditure. They could count money but could not keep the account in writing.

Expressed difficulties in literacy can be seen in this case cited below. In collaboration with the Association of women's information and Co-ordination (AWICO) they were guided to meet their needs in literacy. They sent a note to the women indicating a date for the meeting in their village. They received the letter and realized that the date was the market day and sent another letter changing the date to the next day. As the coordinator of the literacy programme 1 did not receive the letter. We arrived on the planned date and found that all the over twenty members of the group were in the market. They needed to sell their Okra, tomatoes, groundnuts, which was their only source of income. When we met they indicated that it was impossible staying at home on the market day because it comes only once a week. Surprisingly some of them had to leave their articles with their friends to continue selling when they heard that their relative had died.

What is interesting is that their interest in literacy still remains a felt need but was always suppressed by more immediate needs and traditional communal involvements like death celebrations. It should be noted that the meeting with them did hold in the market near their articles of trade. The aim of the meeting was to plan with them on the start of a literacy programme for them. They had much to say. About 90% of those present wanted to know how to write their names, how to record their money, write names on their trade items and also write letters.

During this meeting, there were a few men present most of them literate. After the meeting we had a chat with one of the women who indicated that they allowed the men to join their group because they themselves could not read and write. So the men had to be there to write their minutes and letters. She regretted this fact and said immediately they learn how to read and write the men could be with them but will only play passive roles. The women will write and direct their affairs by themselves.

Women need to be trained as adult literacy instructors. They need special attention especially in rural areas. When women teach others how to read and write, they go deep into their needs, and communication especially matters related to family planning are handled with much more ease than men. They can equally plan in relation to their numerous domestic activities.

The present state of affairs

The government of Cameroon launched an ambitious literacy programme in 2005. This programme focused on the teaching of English to Anglophones and French to francophones is run informally. The experimental phase ended in 2008. The following statistics present the gender situation in both the English and the French speaking zone.

N	Center	Instructor (Sex)	No of learners		Total
			Male	Female	
1	G.S. Obang F.L.C	M	4	44	48
2	G.S. Bujong F.L.C	F	40	4	43
3	G.S. Akossia F.L.C	F	6	2	29
4	P.C. Nchum F.L.C	F	0	19	29
5	P.C. Mankwi F.L.C	M	8	1	23
6	P.C. Asanje F.L.C	M	8	1	26
7	P.S. Agyati F.L.C	M	7	1	17
8	P.S. Mambu F.L.C	M 45	4	2	29
9	G.S. Mbakong F.L.C	M		3	4

				0	8	8	
10	G.S. Tingoh F.L.C	M			5	5	
				1	5		
	GRAND TOTALS				**2**	**3**	
				7	95	42	
	P.C. Bossa F.L.C	M			2	2	
				3	3		
	G.S. Bali Central F.L.C	F			2	2	
				1	1		
	G.S. Fontoh-Mantum F.L.C	F			2	2	
				2	4		
	C.S Bawock F.L.C	F			1	2	
			1	6	7		
	G.S. Mbeluh F.L.C	M			1	2	
				7	6		
	Community Hall Mbufung F.L.C	M			2	2	
				3	5		
	G.S. Wosing F.L.C	M			1	2	
			7	0	7		
		M			1	2	

				6	0	
GRAND TOTAL				1	1	
			5	48	93	

cy Centers and Instructors Per Sub Division Mezam Division Of The Bamend
ogramme.

3: The English zone statistics of 2008

	G.S. Ntoh Bamendakwe F.L.C	M	1	1	5 2	5
	P.S. Ntenfor F.L.C	F	3	1 9	1 2	2
			4	0	7 4	7
	C.S. Ntankah F.L.C	M	4	8	2 2	4
	G.S. Ntingkag	F	3	1 7	1 0	2
	C.S. Ndagh-Mbatu F.L.C	M	4	2	3 6	3
	GRAND TOTAL		1	7	7 8	9

C.S. Futru Nkwen F.L.C	M		5	5	PNA
Women's Hall Mubang F.L.C	M		5	0	PNA
GRAND TOTAL		**5**	**0**	**5**	
G.S. Mbeme Awing F.L.C	M	9	6	5	PNA
G.S. Ntoh- Pinyin F.L.C	F	4	9	3	PNA
G.S. Mbu F.L.C	M	2	2	4	PNA
G.S. Menka F.L.C	M	8	6	4	PNA
G.S. Ntoh-Akum F.L.C	F		2	2	PNA
C.S. Mbei F.L.C	F 49	6	4	0	PNA
G.S. Ntarrah F.L.C	M				PNA

			6	5	1	
	G.S. Mificat-Baligham F.L.C	F	1	3	4	
	G.S. Alatening F.L.C	F	1	1	2	
	P.S. Awing F.L.C	F		1	1	
0	**GRAND TOTAL**		7	89	26	
	G.S. Sabga F.L.C	F	1	0	1	
	G.S. Big Babanki F.L.C	M	5	0	5	
	C.S Hall Bambui F.L.C	M	2	0	2	
	Lih F.L.C	M	5	9	4	
	P.S Atomutoh F.L.C	M	2	0	2	
	Ntekezon F.L.C	F				

			1	8	9	WAY
Timeshul F.L.C	M					PNA
			7	4	1	WAY
C.B.C Chuku F.L.C.	M					PNA
			8	2	0	WAY
GRAND TOTAL			1	63	94	

L= BAFUT + BALI + BAMENDA I + BAMENDA II + BAMENDA III + SANTA
342+193+74+98+55+326+294=**1,382 Learners in Mezam Division**

RENCH ZONE
UA DIVISION

Décembre 2008 Au 24 Mars 2009

French Zone Menoua Division

une	CAF	Date de création	Localisation	No M	No F
	Bamendou I	Juillet 2006	Lekouet Bdou		+
IICHEL	Eppenka M. Bil	Septembre 2005	Ep.GI Penka M. Bil		+
	Ep. Penka M.	Septembre 2005	Ep.GI Penka M.	+	
	CEBEC Baleveng	Juin 2006	Foyer CEBEC		+
	Bassessa	Juillet 2006	Bassessa Djimoki		+
	Motsaletsi	Janvier 2007	Motsa Letsi	+	
-ZEM	Foyer Tsobing	Decembre 2006	Foyer Tsoling	+	
	Saakia Bafou	Août 2006	Saakia Bafou	+	
	Commune Nkongze	Juillet 2006	Commune Nkongze		+

une	CAF	Date de création	Localisation	No

			M	F	M
Ep. Balepé	Septembre 2005	Ep. Balepé	+		07
Kiagmé	Août 2006	Kiagné Baleveng		+	01
Banza	Juillet 2006	Banza Baleveng	+		01
Quartier Housa	Septembre 2005	Fou Masquée	+		08
Tsintué	Octobre 2005	CEBEC Tsintué		+	04
Marché B	Septembre 2005	Marché B			02
Mindjou Tchoundffi	Juillet 2006	Cheferie Mindjou		+	03
Fotsem Lessing	Juillet 2006	Fotsem Lessing		+	04
Foto Kemwaa	Septembre 2005	Face MEC	+		10

par Supervision
mbre 2008 Au 24 Mars 2009

CAF	Date de création	Localisation	Nombre d'		
			M	F	M
Nsui Foto	Juillet 2006	Coté UCB		+	02
Gic	Novembre 2007	Face MEC	+		19

	Balevoni	Juillet 2007	Balevoni	+
		Août 2006		+
	Santchou I	Septembre 2005	Santchou Ville	+
	Ep. Meket Fondonera	Juillet 2006	Ep. Meket	+
:HOU	Santchou II	Juin 2006	Santchou Ville	+
TONGO	Lotsa Village	Janvier 2007	Foyer Lotsa	-

CAF par Supervision
6 Décembre 2008 Au 24 Mars 2009

iune	CAF	Date de création	Localisation	N	
				M	F
	Ep. Fomopéa	Août 2006	Ep.Fomopea		+
)UE	Ep. Fontso Toualo	Septembre 2005	Ep.Fontsa T.	+	
	Bamendou	Septembre 2005	Foyer Bamegwou		+
	Fotomena	Juillet 2006	Foyer Tchuelessong		+

TOTAL				17

istics of the National Literacy Programme In Mezam Division Of The North W
Language)

Gender analysis

Out of the 43 centres in the division, 16 are run by women representing 37.2% of the instructors. Only one third of the instructors are hence women. Out of 1,382 learners, only 190 are male and 1,192 are women. The male represent only 13.7% of the learners.

These figures indicate that 86.3% of those in the literacy classes in this division are women. This is close to the data from the Menoua division of the West region.

If we agree that the illiteracy problem in the world is essentially under developing countries' problems and women's problems, then the high percentage of women in adult literacy classes simply confirms this tendency. If we believe equally that the males equally dominate over the women even in areas that essentially concern them, then this data equally confirms that 63.8% of male instructors teach 86.3% female learners while 37.2% of female teach 13.7% males. The reverse would have reflected a more gender balance perspective.

Table 4: Gender distribution of Literacy Tutors for the Mezam Division

	Instructors	%	Learners	%
Male	27	62.7	190	13.7%
Female	16	37.2	192	86.3%

Gender imbalance

If we subtract 37.2 percent of the existing female instructors from the supposed 86.3 percent of the participants who are women (the supposed female instructors percentage) then we will realise that about (13) 50 percent of the existing male teachers are supposed to be replaced by females to create a gender balance. When this gender balance is created and men encouraged and trained to run male literacy classes, we have a possibility of having more male learners coming to literacy classes. This is evident in the fact that many male oriented groups exist where women do not have access. Real functional literacy in an essentially gender sensitive context like Africa must be gender sensitive. That is the case with the Ghana experience (see below).

Critical Evaluation

Objectives and organization of the National Literacy Programme: Mezam Division, (North West Region of Cameroon)

The project is aimed at teaching basic literacy (reading and writing skills) in English and numeracy skills to illiterates. It is aimed at initial learning with an achievement level less than the first school-leaving certificate. Its focus is to cause the learners to love education. If they develop the love for education, they can go ahead by themselves and equally encourage their children. They generally meet two or three times a week on a two hours basis. They run two or three levels and a change from one level to the other comes when they notice an improvement in participation. There is a graduation ceremony at the end but no certificates awarded. The meetings hold mostly in primary school premises.

(1) Difficulties, Sight and location

Since most of the participants are old, they have sight problems. They need eyeglasses which they cannot provide for themselves and which the project is not providing. There is a need for adaptable approaches to teach them while waiting for a possibility of acquiring eyeglasses. The scanty and dispersed settlement in the mountainous relief of the North West Region means that learners have to make long distances to classes. When we notice that women usually carry the burden of child bearing (and at times child upbringing) alone, distance trekking to literacy classes could play very negatively on their performance. Bringing the classes closer to women and probably inserting them into their existing female social gatherings reduces the number of meetings to attend and hence more time to rest.

(2) Finance and equipment

Nforbi, (2003) identified finance as the first priority for literacy in Cameroon. In the National Literacy Programme, the long-term financial vision was not certain. The project launched in 2005 had 2008 as the end of the experimental phase. Each instructor got 20 000 FRS (about US $40) as monthly incentive. Unfortunately, this incentive could not go beyond the first phase. As of may 2009, no incentive had come in since the start of 2009.

The management of finances of this first phase had the following weaknesses:

a) Absence of income generating projects (IGPs)

From the statistics, a majority of the participants are women. It would have been ideal to create Women in Literacy and Development Department in the project. As such, appropriate income generating projects would have been created to enable sustainability. In the absence of finance at the start of this second phase, the project would have had proceeds from the IGPs sustaining the project.

b) Top-bottom management approach

The management of the budget dictated from above did not take into consideration the contribution of the local supervisors. For instance a large centre with several assistant instructors involved, needs more incentives than a centre with fewer learners run by one instructor.

Women are known as better financial managers in Africa. A National programme which aims at reducing illiteracy with women constituting a great target needed women in high management positions which is not the case.

c) Equipment

The National office of the programme has a four wheel drive vehicle and a bus. The zonal supervisors have a transport allowance, while the divisional supervisors have motor bikes and the instructors have bicycles. Women in this area are generally not used to riding bikes and bicycles. In fact one of the instructors in the Ndian division said a canoe would have been more adapted than a bicycle since he needs to cross streams to his centres.

d) Communication

This seems to be a major setback in this programme. Women though constituting a major population of the learners have not participated in decision-making. It should be noted that we are dealing with women who are matured and active in life. Their opinion in running the next phase of this programme is crucial. In fact involving women as actors in literacy programmes is a better way of empowering them. Most of those involved in the management of the Summer Institute of Linguistics (SIL) and Cameroon association for Bible translation and literacy (CABTAL) are women. Most of these women are foreigners from the developed countries showing a higher awareness in women empowerment than the under developed world.

Content of Learner's Manual: Level I and II

The existing manual for the programme is built on the teaching of vowel and consonant sounds. It is hence focused on helping the learners to spell words and write them. It is not built on a functional approach which can empower the learners. The absence of functionality is clear and can be an indicator for the failure of the programme in the long run if nothing is done. One of the requirements of the second phase should be the introduction of functional projects like in the Ghanaian experiences discussed in the second part of this paper.

Levels of Education of the Instructors

Only 23 percent of the teachers are above first school leaving certificate. The level of education of the instructors does not permit them to take the learners above the basic level. For the National literacy programme to be functional there is need to aim at going above the basic level. This will imply recruiting more people with a minimum of advanced level and training them on functional literacy through a well set up instructor's, training programme scientifically certified by a related University Department.

Statistics of the Menoua Division of the West region under the (Nkongsamba Pole of the National Literacy programme (French language)

Table 4 presents statistics of the national literacy program in another pole in the francophone region. Here French is taught to francophones as opposed to English taught to anglophones in the first data.

Here we have 29 centres with 29 instructors in the Menoua Division of west region which falls under the Nkongsamba Pole. Fourteen (14) of the 29 instructors are female representing 48.2%. Out of the 1,125 learners, 934 are females representing 84.8% of the learners.

Table 5: Gender Table

	Instructor	%	Learners	%
Male	13	31.7	171	15.2
Female	14	48.2	954	84.8

Although with an 84.8% female attendance, only 48.2% of the instructors are women. To create a gender balance, 36.6% of the male instructors need to be replaced by females.

Comparative Study Of The Two Poles: Mezam In The Bamenda Pole (English) And Menoua In The Nkongsamba Pole (French)

The first striking similarity is the percentage of the female learners, which is above 80% in the two poles. This confirms the fact that the illiteracy problem in Africa is essentially a woman's problem, and needs to be tackled with a gender consciousness.

The role of women in this very sensitive domain is felt only in the inferior position. Their presence is highly felt at the disadvantaged position. This can lead to the erroneous belief that women are more active in the literacy centres than men. The contrary is true. They are over 80% more passive than men since they are only acted upon and do not have a voice in decision making and implementation.

It should be noted that more effort is being put in to meet the above challenges in the Menoua Division than in the Mezam Division. The number of female instructors is higher than those of the Mezam pole. Their programme has approaches that are more functional and there is a variety of material to teach the learners; different functional lessons, problem charts, learners' manuals and teachers' manuals are available. A majority of the centres in the Mezam pole are located in school premises while those in the Menoua Division are diversified; community halls, council halls, village meeting halls and school halls. This diversification of locations has a possibility of bringing the centres closer to the learners.

The rest of the problems like finance and equipment are equally the same in the Menoua Division. We can conclude that even though the National literacy programme is going through the evaluation phase of the experimental phase that started in 2005, it needs to consider amongst others the gender issue in its next phase.

The Ghana Experience

The Language Situation

Ghana has about 60 mother tongues. About 15 are used at the national level. They are taught in schools from primary to university divided between 7 regions of Ghana.

These languages are chosen officially by the state. Children who go to school from primary to secondary have a possibility of speaking and writing one or two of these languages depending in which region of Ghana they find themselves. Learning to read and write the mother tongue in school facilitates the learning of the official language. It should be noted that people have accepted these choices of the government. People are simply learning it as a tradition, although they still use their mother tongues in day-to-day activities.

These languages chosen by the state are gradually serving as trade languages. People express themselves in the markets, churches, and in the streets. In the Volta Region for instance, people speak Ewe and use it in churches and markets even though they have their own languages. In Hohoe, the capital of the Volta Region, the neighbouring villages have their own mother tongues like Tumuli and Selee. Since only Ewe is written and taught and is the language of Power, they use it in church and in the market. In the streets of Accra, the languages spoken are Ga and Ewe and Ga dominates. There are about 8 institutions offering mother-tongue literacy.

Literacy programmes

The Ghana institute of linguistics, literacy and Bible translation (GILLBT)

GILBERT operates in six regions of Ghana and over 31 language projects in 1999. There are regional coordinators who take care of about 4 projects each. Each project has a project coordinator, a paid supervisor and voluntary supervisors. We equally have the literacy animators or facilitators who teach the learners. This programme is organised in three stages: basic, advanced and bridge.

The basic stage is for those who are just starting literacy work. The adults attend classes once or twice a week and each section takes two hours. Classes hold in the evenings from 8 to 10 PM. Since most of these classes are in the rural area, there is a serious problem of lighting. Lanterns are however provided but the problem of fuel remains an obstacle.

Statistics of the GILLBT Literacy Programme in the North-Ghana for the Basic stage:

1. West Dagbani

Table 6: Statistics of the GILLBT Literacy Programme.

Zone	Voluntary teacher		No of schools	No Class	Basic learner	
	Male	Female			Male	Female
Nwodua	12	1	12	17	132	148
Cheyohi	6	/	5	6	63	57
Tamale	2	/	2	4	43	47
Kpaligun	9	/	7	10	191	133
Gbangong	5	/	10	6	70	60
Ligbin zergu	4	/	4	5	35	49
Jekpatti	2	/	2	8	46	33
Jima	9	/	4	4	60	29
Moglaa	10	/	4	11	136	61
Kumbugu	11	/	9	13	140	114
Kasuhyili	8	/	7	10	103	55
Garizegu	1	5	9	13	176	56
Total	93	6	109	109	1195	862

2. East Dagbani

Zone	Voluntary teacher		No of schools	No Class	Basic learner	
	Male	Female			Male	Female
Adibo	10	2	7	11	121	104
Malizeri	14	/	9	14	203	103
Kpalgighini	6	/	5	6	78	45
LUgu	1	/	1	1	17	13
Sambu	1	/	1	1	16	14
Bimbila	4	/	3	5	20	7
Gushugu	12	2	11	14	138	169
Sang	9	/	9	9	371	39
Total	57	4	46	61	966	494

Even though it is evidently clear from statistics at the National level that there more women illiterates in Ghana than men, the statistics in the literacy classes do not confirm this. This is because the northern part of Ghana is an essentially Muslim region where women's roles are felt more at home than in public. In spite of the high female illiteracy rates, fewer women than men attend these literacy classes. However, these zones are essentially Muslim confirming the high degree of female illiteracy as shown in other Muslim countries in Sub Sahara Africa.

Just like in the northern part of Cameroon which is an essentially Muslim region, the male are more present at the implementation level 150 as against 8 female as facilitators. In the literacy classes, we have 2161 male and 1356 women-making a total of 3517 learners. Here the women constitute a very high percentage as learners as opposed to the 5.3% they occupy as instructors

The creation of a Women's in Literacy Development (WILD) department was a solution to this gender imbalance in this project as seen in the paper

Advanced stage

At this stage, the post primers are used. Topics related to health, agriculture, environmental studies are treated. The learners equally meet in the evening from 8 to 10 PM. It takes a period of one year for the learners to go through the programme. Testing for the advanced certificate focuses on fluency.

Bridge

After the basic and the advanced certificate on the mother tongue, the learners can now get to a stage of transition into English, which is the official language. The first part of this stage focuses on oral English while reading in advanced material continues in the mother tongue. Evaluation at this level consists of the following;

- Answering questions in the second language equivalent to oral material;
- Creative writing in the mother tongue.

The second part of the bridge programme is directed towards completing transitional primers, which introduce the sound system of the second language.

Adult primary schools are intended for those who have completed basic and advanced certificates. The classes hold in the dry season when farmers do not have much work to do. The main aim of the adult primary school is to bridge the learners into junior secondary schools, adult vocational institutions and subsequently senior secondary schools.

Non formal education department of the ministry of education of Ghana (NFED)

NFED runs a nationwide functional adult literacy programme based on the mother tongue. This programme that started in 1984 carved the country into 16 literacy zones with zonal supervisors. Facilitators are recruited and trained for the various zones. Each group had about 25 to 30 learners. A facilitator takes a group from the beginning to the end of the one to two years period.

National Functional Literacy Programme, Ghana, Statistics on Learners Enrolled Completed and Drop Outs: Batches 1-8, 1992 – 2002

Table 7: National Functional literacy programme, Ghana

Regions	Recruited			Graduates			Drop-outs			% Drop-outs	% Of female enrolled
	Male	Female	Total	Male	Female	Total	Male	Female	Total		
Ashanti	66832	137361	204199	56762	108232	164994	9927	29005	38932	19%	67.2%
Brong Ahafo	79265	91098	170363	67545	100946	168491	13164	11929	27093	15.9%	53.4%
Central	56515	94701	131216	42626	86708	129634	13889	8000	21889	14.4%	62.6%
Eastern	73163	135451	208614	61908	121317	183223	11255	14134	23389	12.17%	64.9%
Greater Accra	19272	47056	66328	12495	34268	46763	6777	12788	19565	29.4%	70.9%
Northern	112749	80241	192990	93538	68494	162032	19211	11747	30958	16%	41.5%
Upper East	54066	64495	118561	47567	48339	96106	64996	15956	22455	11.6%	54.3%
Upper West	72207	67785	139992	63652	54605	118257	85550	13180	21735	15.5%	48.4%
Volta	65876	159096	224972	53286	145051	198337	12590	14045	26635	11.8%	70.7%
Western	67485	125321	192806	53837	100975	154812	13648	24346	37994	19.7%	64.9%
General total	667430	1002605	1670035	649915	847475	1397390	117515	155130	272645	16.3%	60%

The statistics of 10 years in Ghana indicate that in overall, we have 60% of women who enrolled in literacy classes. 60.6% of the graduate during this period was women. Even though the Greater north region has the highest female enrolment of 70.9%, 65.3% of the overall 29.4% dropouts in this region are women and 56.8% of the overall dropouts are female.

In the Northern region, 41.5% of those enrolled are women. This figure reflects those of the GILLBT literacy programme in the Dagbani zone in this region. Here we are faced with a cultural reality just like in the upper west region. The northern regions of Cameroon and Ghana share the same cultural heritage which is essentially Muslim. Culturally the women are more concerned with household and family care than outdoor activities. Bringing literacy closer home and training women as facilitators is necessary to meet these cultural challenges.

The Controversy

If we consider literacy as an important activity for economic development, then we should as well address issues related to literacy management and gender. In relation to this, a local literacy committee with a gender consciousness might be preferred to a central body, which is not very directly related to the management of finances. We are saying in other words that the problem at stake is that women should be given the chance to be literacy animators as well as manage literacy funds. The GILLBT system succeeded on a voluntary based approach because they were able to train animators who taught at will – a good number of them women. Some of these animators joined the NFED programmes which pay better. This is a clear indication that even though they taught on a voluntary basis, they were waiting for a moment when they would receive something better. This same experience was observed in Cameroon during the first phase of the National Literacy Programme. Instructors abandoned CABTAL voluntary classes for this programme.

The Ghana Institute Of Literacy, Linguistics And Bible Translation (The GILLBT) Experience

A realistic experience of GILLBT is the creation of the women in literacy and development (WILD) department. Creating a women department in a literacy programme empowers them. It had been established that women's needs are not the same as those of men. Women therefore need literacy programmes adapted to their realities as well as primers which handle issues of interest like gender and child care. There is need therefore to organize their classes when they are free since they have much to do in the family. More important, is the fact that most of our communities are patriarchal where women and men would not cope together in class work. Women are therefore encouraged in the GILLBT programme to take part in writer's workshop where they come out with material of their own needs. GILLBT proposes the following for active involvement of women in literacy:

- Involvement of women as members of the language committee,

- Involvement of female participants in training courses as well as designing some of these courses specifically for them.
- Involve women in leadership and managerial positions within literacy projects.
- Encourage women to come out with income generating projects which can help them to cater for the needs of their family.

Income generating projects

Even though GILLBT projects depend highly on foreign donors, much is being done to put into place local projects, which can in the long run generate income for self-funding. IGPS are therefore a very important component of the programme. IGPS are therefore funded as part of the overall literacy and development programme for the following objectives found in GILLBT guidelines for IGPS 1999.
- To give experience in small and medium scale income generating activities;
- To afford communities the opportunity to develop managerial and entrepreneurial skills;
- To help communities raise funds to support individual literacy projects;
- To help literacy projects relate literacy to community based projects.
- To encourage both men and women to work together and develop a sense of self confidence;
- To serve as a base for communities to work towards financial autonomy for each literacy projects.

In order to realize these objectives, training courses are organized on participatory rural appraisal techniques as a means of identifying promising IGPS that will be community based. Their trainings are given on financial management, which includes loans and repayments. The language committee identifies the IGP and proposes it to the IGPS and development coordinator of the literacy and development department. This department in collaboration with the language committee studies and assesses the project to see its utility to the community before granting the funds of which 50% is refundable.

This effort is yielding a lot of fruits as a good number of women groups are able to run micro-projects which enable them to take care of the daily needs of their family as they progress in literacy. Some literacy projects are equally able to raise money from the projects (like the Dagbani project in Northern Ghana) whose sales go a long way to support the project.

Similarities and differences between literacy programmes in Cameroon and Ghana

In terms of similarities, these two countries all share English as an official language and hence one colonial experience. They are all conscious of the gender problem in literacy. Non-governmental organizations are involved in their literacy programmes.

In Cameroon, the National Association of Cameroonian language Committees (NACALCO) and the Cameroon Association for bible translation and literacy CABTAL are involved in mother – tongue literacy. GILLBT in Ghana plays the same role. In these two countries, they collaborate with government organizations fighting illiteracy.

As far as differences are concerned, the Bilingual and highly multilingual nature of Cameroon poses a bigger challenge of literacy than Ghana. The experience of Ghana shows that they are more advanced in solving the gender problem. The existence of a women's department in their literacy programme called women in literacy and development (WILD) is a case in point. This department has set up income generating projects (IGPs) which can combat the funding problem; The WILD department in GILLBT Ghana has created greater gender awareness in the Ghanaian literacy programme than in Cameroon. Women are taking managerial and animation roles and hence empowering the other women. The creation of a women's department in literacy programmes is hence an imperative. The creation of a women's empowerment ministry in Cameroon is a step ahead to solve this problem of gender imbalance. Instead of linking literacy to youth affairs, it will be better to link it to the women's empowerment ministry in Cameroon since the illiteracy problem in Cameroon and Africa in general is more a women's problem.

Conclusion

Literacy activities in Africa reflect the Chauvinist penchant in the continent. At the decision-making and implementational level, the male dominate. The female who are in a majority victim of illiteracy fill the literacy classes as participants. They are taught essentially by men who do not master their predicaments. A majority of the illiterate male who are not used to sitting with women in the same meeting do not come to the literacy classes. Granting gender sensitive classes will solve this problem. Besides learning from the Ghanaian experience of WILD, Cameroonians need to improve on the financial situation and salvage literacy programmes in the continent.

Cameroon and Ghana have the experience and expertise needed to improve on its National (adult) literacy programme from a gender perspective. The women need to be trained to play key roles in literacy in Africa.

References

Barbara, Trudell. (2003), "The impact of Mother Tongue education in the Bafut, Kom, and Nso' communities of Northwest Cameroon. SIL

Bangbose, A. (ed.), (1976), Mother Tongue Education: The West African Experience. UNESCO, Paris

Bhola, H.S. (1984). Campaigning for Literacy: Eight National Experiences of the Twentieth Century with a Memorandum to Decision Makers, Paris.

Boadi, L. (1978). "Mother Tongue Education in Ghana", in Bamgbose, A.(ed) Mother Tongue Education: The West African Experience

Bongasu, T.K. (1995). "Language Problems in Anglophone Cameroon: Present Writers and future Readers in Ntsobe A.M et al (1985) (ed) Sosongo

Brian, V.S. (1984). "Literacy in Theory and Practice" *in Cambridge studies in oral and written culture 9,* Cambridge: Cambridge University Press.

Carrol, B (1976), "The nature of the reading process" in singer, M and Rudidith (eds), Theoretical models and processes of Reading. International Reading Association Newmark.

Chia, N, Emmanuel and Nsawir KEtheldreda (2003) "Adult literacy: A survey of the south West Region" AJAL N° 3 Yaoundé

Chumbow, B.S. (1980). "Language and Language Policy in Cameroon," in Ndira t.t (ed) An African experiment in Nation building: The Bilingual Cameroon Republic since Reunification, westview Press, Boulder, Colorado.

Dunnigan, L. (1989). *Mother tongue literature in Cameroon: A language planning perspective,* unpublished maîtrise memoire.University of Yaoundé. Yaoundé

Linda, D. (1989). *Mother Tongue Literacy in Cameroon. A Language Planning Perspective.* Unpublished Maîtrise Memoire. University of Yaoundé. Yaoundé

Marcella, B. (1992). 'Women and Literacy'. *United Nations Non-Governmental Liaison Service,* Red Books Ltd. London.

Margaret, S.T. (1992). *The Role of Language Committees in Developing the indigenous language of Cameroon,* unpublished masters' thesis, University of Texas at Arlington

Mba. G. Et Chiatoh. B (2000) "Current trends and perspectives for mother tongue in Cameroon" AJAL N° 1 Yaoundé.

Nanfah, G. (2003). Analyse contrastive des parlers Yemba du département de la Menoua de l'ouest Cameroun. Doctorate thesis, Université de Cologne

Nforbi E (2001) "The challenges of the basic standardisation process of minority African Languages: Case study of Mfumte Cameroon and Selee Ghana" in *African journal of applied Linguistics* (AJAL N° 2, Tadadjeu M and Mutaka N, ed, Yaoundé.

Nforbi E (2005). "Community Involvement in Mother Tongue Education through a Dynamic Functional Language Committee" in AJAL N° Yaoundé (47-61).

Nforbi, E (2003). *In Search of an adult literacy model for Cameroon.* Unpublished Doctorate thesis

Nforbi, E (2006). "Efforts and challenges involved in establishing an adult literacy model for Cameroon" *in African linguistics and the development of African Communities.* CHIA Emmanuel, ed. CODESRIA Book Series Dakar.

Sharwood Smith, M, (1994), *Second language learning: Theoretical foundations languages,* London and New York

Stringer, M.D. and N.G Faradas, (2000). *Working together for literacy*. SIL, Yaoundé

Tadadjeu, M (1996). A model for Functional Trilingual Education Planning in Africa,

Tadadjeu M, Sadembouo E, and Mbah M (2004) Pédagogie des Langues Maternelles Africaines. Edition CLA. Yaoundé.

Tadadjeu M. (1997) *A New Approach to Adult Education in Cameroon* Paper presented at UNESCO's 5th International Conference on Adult Education. Hamburg July 14-17, 1997.

Tchamda, F.M. (3rd edition). *Qu'est-ce que NUFI ?* SOPECAM, Yaoundé.

UNESCO (1970). *Functional Literacy: Why and How*. Paris.

UNESCO (2005). "Links between the Global Initiatives in Education". Education for Sustainable Development in Action, Technical Paper No.1. Paris: UNESCO.

UNESCO Institute for Statistics (2006, re-edition). *International Standard Classification of Education (ISCED 1997)*. Montreal: UNESCO Institute for Statistics.

UNESCO Institute for statistics (2008). International Literacy Statistics: A review of concepts, Methodology and current data. Montreal

Willmot, Patrick (1980). Ideology and National Consciousness. Ibadan: Lantern books.

Section C:
Representing Gender in Context

5

English Pedagogic Materials as Robust Vector of Gendering

Paul Mbangwana & Alice Tangang
University Of Yaoundé I

Language and Gender

Bauer (2006) asserts that language does not only reflect and foster sexist attitudes; it is seen to actively contribute to the construction of sexist social reality which are traditional cultural practices. It will be instructive to examine how certain social attitudes and traditional practices have been encoded and recycled in English school manuals for pupils and students in the nursery, primary and secondary schools in the French sub-system of education in Cameroon.

An educational environment, like the school institutions, has the duty to mould their learners morally, academically, linguistically and especially culturally and socially. Pupils and students are by nature receptive to the pedagogic materials that teachers use to teach them. These teaching materials offer opportunities to develop learners' awareness in relation to gender roles, identities and issues pertaining there from in the society. Subservient roles for the female and male roles of high consideration need to be revisited in this our day of age.

Culture and Gender

Traditional practices focus on maintaining and producing particular gender relationships between males and females. Many of the English manuals for pupils and students in the French sub-system of education in Cameroon seem to convey a mistaken idea that they are being used only as pedagogic aids to mould the learner academically and linguistically. They forget that these language manuals also serve as vectors for moulding the learners socially and culturally at such a tender age when these young learners are in their critical formative development. Such a learning process takes place unconsciously and effectively. Many of the scenic illustrations for conversation, pair work and group activities should appropriately and purposefully be conceived. If these traditional language discourses are thoughtlessly conceived, as it is the case in certain of the English school manuals for French-speaking pupils and students, the result will be the perpetuation of the time-honoured gender bias of traditional practices and values wherein the female is confined to family chores (see Atanga 2007) and the male works freely in the public domain as economic resource and producer of scientific and technological knowledge. Yet the school should play the revolutionary change that the present society is called upon to effect. A good number of traditional roles need to be deconstructed and reconstructed so that a balance of gender roles can be enhanced and guaranteed. English school manuals have a professional obligation to be well conceived before they are written and illustrated. What they impress on the young learners is not just the English vocabulary and structural expressions but more importantly the ideas and attitudes that mould them and forge a worldview for them. When school manuals codify these traditional divisions of gender roles and practices, the learners are seen rehearsing them without a second thought as they go through their linguistic exercises. Krashen (1975) in *de Bot et al* (2005:35) reminds us that people do not learn a language only by studying the rules of grammar but also by 'experiencing enough meaningful input and communication within that language'. Ideas expressed in these English language manuals are unconsciously assimilated. This is more noticeable in our patriarchal society where language reflects and reinforces gender roles and relations. This is in keeping with Sapir-Whorfian hypothesis which asserts that language is not just a means of communication; it also portrays our cultural values and thought patterns including the shaping of our perception of reality as we see the world in the categories of our language. The disturbing situation is that the knowledge embedded in culture is constructed to forge gendered division of occupations in the manuals. Bearing this in mind one wonders why textbook writers who use imaginativeness to sharpen learners' language communicative skills seem at the same time to be insensitive to the division of gender roles and identities which are essentially bias against the female where the male is visible everywhere and the female playing either negative or subservient roles.

Objective of investigation

The aim of this study is to examine the gender issues and traditional division of gender roles and identities recurrent in the school manuals which are replete with conservative traditional discourses, displaying women and girls as caretakers, cooks, baby-sitters, shoppers, lovers and many other inferior roles, (see pictures 8,10,22), (also Atanga 2010 forthcoming) while those of men and boys are knowledgeable scientists, inventors, adventurers, providers of wealth and owners of things of high money value as can be gleaned from pictures 5,6,7,9.

Gender and identity

Morton (2000) in Ellis and Barkhuizen (2005:285) sees social identity as 'the multiple ways in which people understand themselves in relation to others.' Learning a language amounts to learning to be a member of a particular culture as social order is reproduced through language. Many cultures make a distinction between the roles men and women are subjected to in the society. When young learners learn a language they take into consideration the cultural roles assigned to them on the basis of their sex. Coates (1989:122) further explains that in the process of learning to become 'linguistically competent, young learners learn to be a full-fledged male or female member of the speech community'. When young learners adjust linguistic behaviour to their sex, like females confining themselves to family domestic chores they create and foster gender identities. In the various discourses here and there in the school manuals, pupils and students interact socially in school settings. It is precisely during these interactions that social and gender identities of learners are constructed unconsciously.

Method for data collection and analysis

Data collection

Data for this study was obtained essentially from three series of school manuals which are used in teaching and learning of English in the French sub-system of education in Cameroon, for example: *Go for English* from 1-7, *Champions in English* from 1-6, and *Evans Cameroon primary English* from 1-6.

Picture 1

Content of the manuals

These school manuals lend themselves to a wide variety of conversation exercises, of reading, listening and grammar texts through which the learners' sensitivity to gendered discourses is perceived. These young learners within the formal school environment are nursery, primary, and secondary school pupils and students, respectively. Their ages range from 3-16 years. The texts respond to the codified traditional gendered discourses in which traditional division of roles and identities are enshrined in linguistic structures which the young learners rehearse.

The manuals use various occupational and vocational activities to reproduce traditional practices and beliefs (ideologies) which help to socialise the learners in gender roles, relationships and gender division of labour (see Sunderland 2004).

Illustrations and analysis.

Use will be made of figures, pictures and tables to analyse the issues under study

A linguistic analysis of the textbook materials will make use of concordance techniques to show various themes and their recurrent associations to male and female subjects.

Caroll and Kowitz in Sunderland (1994) demonstrate that frequency counts, distributional and collocational analyses can be used to highlight certain undertones of gender saliency in contexts where gendering is covertly stated. This is because, for example, distributional analysis may be signalling a normal or bias occurrence, a relative frequency of an item may be an indicator of gender saliency, key word in context (KWIC) concordances may help to examine key words in reference to collocational semantic implications.

Issues and discussions

Distributional analysis

Using distributional analysis of certain items to the exclusion of others may be an indication of a hidden gender bias. Let us see how in ***Go for English*** Book 7, high status, inventions, great personalities and professions are associated to male figures in a single manual as can be judged from the following events and personalities:

Table 1

Names	Events
Yuri Alexeyevich Gagarin	first man in space
Apollo II	moon launch
Alexi Leonov	first person to walk in space
Neil Armstrong	makes his first step to the moon
Malthus	population theory
Galileo Kepler and Isaac Newton	solar system
Nelson Mandela	first black president in South Africa
Dr. Joseph Devine	an aspect of fresh water organisms
Dr. Lyle Campbell	a linguist
Youssou N'Dour	renown successful musician
Carl Weinberg and Robert Williams	scientists of solar energy

Mutangangi Kacolho	metal forging
Mr. Kitan	a successful banker
James Watson and Francis Drick	discovered the structure of DNA
Sister Helen Prejean	a 55 year old Roman Catholic nun
Mrs. Dolu	a crane operator
Mrs. Gondo	looks after the family

These personalities and events highlight the inventive and professional status and achievements of male figures which dominate the scene with their exploratory manipulation of the physical environment. Women appear just in those low station and invisible vocations like nun, crane operator and caretakers of the family.

Another area of limited worldview for the female can be seen in *Champions in English* CM2 (book 6): 16 where Mrs. Baba is apportioning assignments to her children.

Picture 2

While Mamadou and Arouna are going about their outdoor pursuits Aissatou is confined to domestic work. This can be discerned in the conversation in picture 2.

Mamadou and Arouna are good at paddling the canoe and shepherding the goats, respectively, Aissatou is good at drying fish and Mrs. Baba selling fish.

Mrs. Walker is presented as a shopper in Oxford where she moves from various shops: clothes shop, toy shop, hat shop, shoe shop, baker's, newsagent's, butcher's, greengrocer's while her husband Mr. Walker is professor of mathematics at the University of Oxford.

Champions in English CE2 (book 4): 59-60

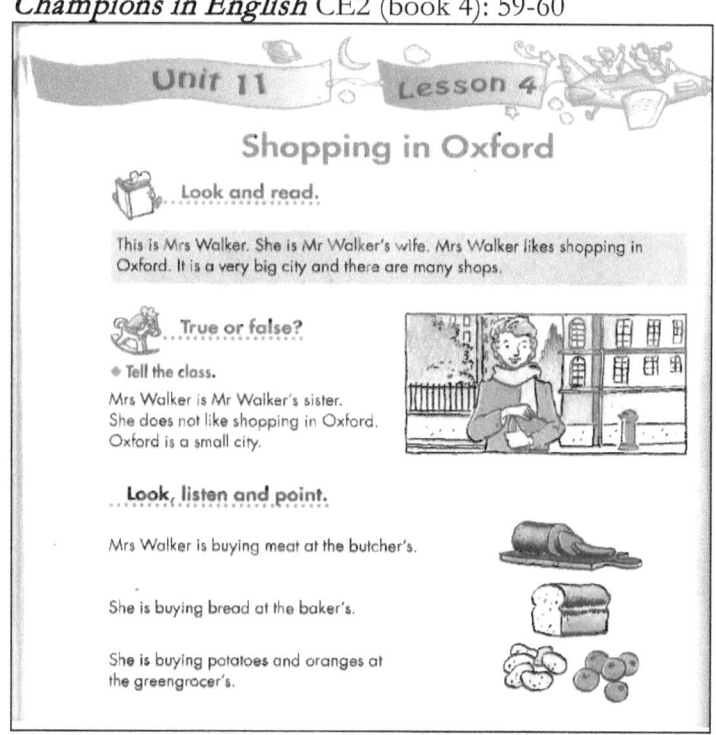

Picture 3

Read and answer.

I am Mr Walker. I am English. I live in Oxford, England. I am a professor at the University. I teach Mathematics. Oxford is a beautiful city. There are many old buildings. Many famous people studied at the University of Oxford.

Where does Mr Walker come from?
Where does he live?
Where does he teach Mathematics?
Where is Oxford? Point to it on the map.
What can you see in Oxford?
What did many famous people do in Oxford?

Picture 4

Champions in English CM2: (book 6):23 and 57

A health visit. Women as nurses and men and co-pilots and women as
as doctors
handlers on the plane.

Men as pilots

luggage

Picture 5

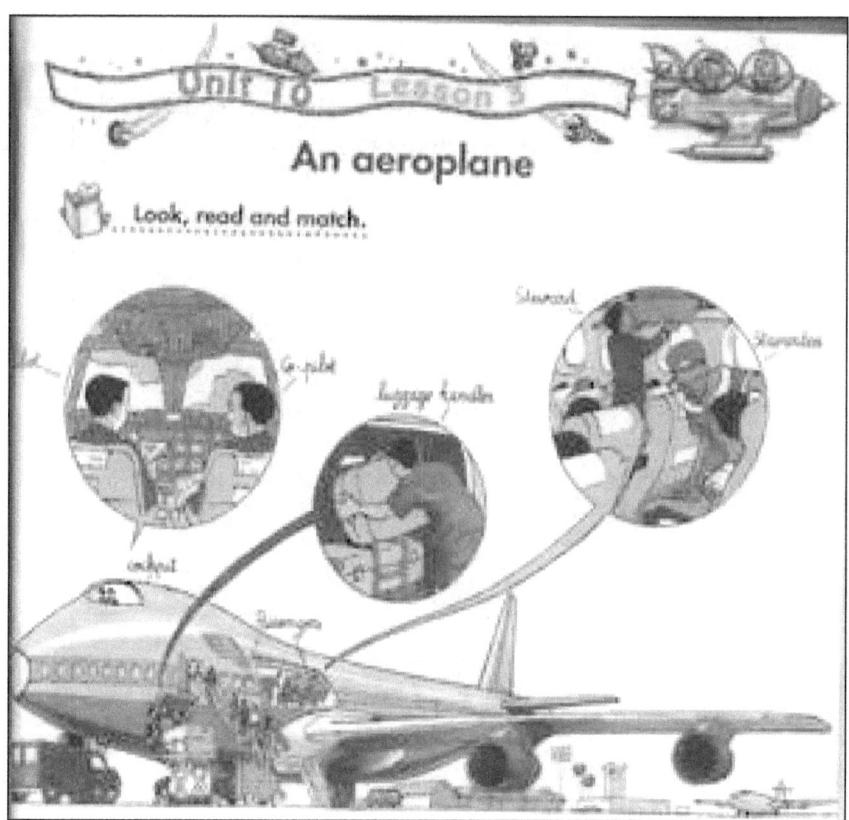

Picture 6

Picture 7: Champions in English CM1(book5):64-65 - Paul as maker of a wooden bicycle while Elisabeth is a server of coffee

Picture 8

Boys own dogs, horses, hens, cats and cows. Girls own oranges, pineapples and tangerines.
SIL (nursery):62-63

Picture 9

Picture 10

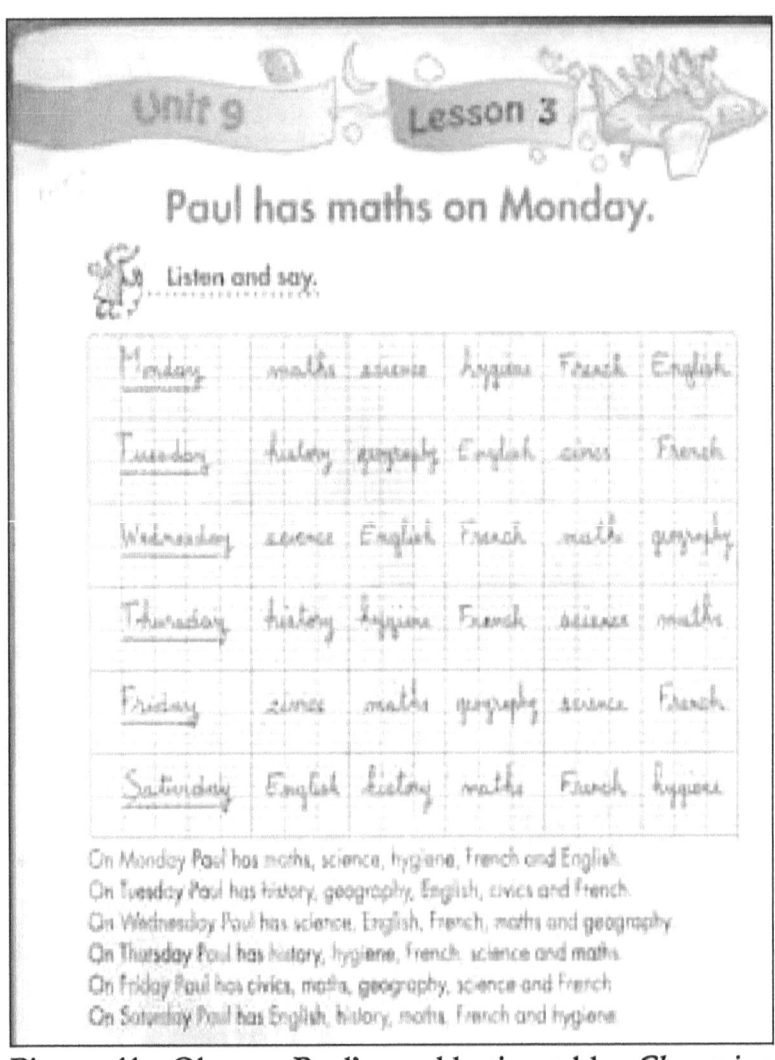

Picture 11: Observe Paul's weekly timetable, *Champions in English* CE1 (book3): 44 and Mrs. Fouda's weekly domestic diary CE2 (book 4):24.

Picture 12

While Paul outlines his daily subjects to study from Monday to Saturday, Mrs. Fouda spells out her domestic chores and some outings. This can be detailed as follows: Monday: buys mangoes and guavas, Tuesday: goes to the market, Wednesday: washes clothes, Thursday: cleans the house, Friday: goes to the mosque, Saturday: goes to town, Sunday: visits a friend. CE2(Book 4): 46, 48, 49, 50.

Picture 13

Picture 14

Picture 15

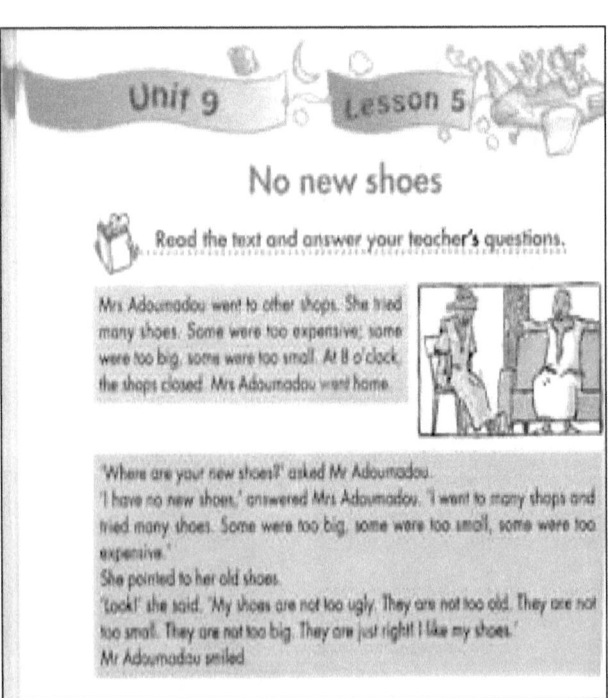

Picture 16

Pictures 13, 14, 15, 16. Demonstrate the plight of Mrs. Adoumadou who needs a new pair of shoes. She tells her husband and then goes shopping in town. Telling her husband insinuates the subservient dependency of women on their husbands. She finds beautiful black shoes, which she likes but they are too expensive. She has to move to a second shop where she sees a red pair of shoes, which is not too expensive, but it is too small for her. As she moves to the next shop the story is still the same: some are too expensive, some are too small and the others are too big. Finally the shops close at 8 pm and she goes back home without a new pair of shoes. Indeed she needed to buy where it is cheapest and not where the quality is the major concern.

Even when it comes to simple practical things like cycling and giving information on finding directions the male demonstrates mastery of them (see picture17) and the female's incompetence is shown as she makes many mistakes with traffic regulations (picture 18).

Picture 17: Male and female cycling. CM1(Book5): 41-42.

Picture 18

> *1*
>
> ## Reading: Finding the way
>
> Before you read the conversation, talk to your friend about where you live. Give your friend directions from school to your house.
>
>
>
> Stranger: Excuse me please, can you tell me the way to the D.O.'s office?
> Mary: It is easy. Take the second turn on your right. The D.O.'s office is after the market. You can't miss it.
> John: No, that's not right. You won't find the market or the D.O.'s office if you take the second turn. Take the third and ask when you get to the market.
> Mary: I am sorry. I made a mistake. It's not the second turn. It is the third turn on the right. Thank you, John.
> Stranger: If I may ask, is the Post Office near the D.O.'s office?
> Mary: Not really, but it is within walking distance. As soon as you come out of the D.O.'s office you'll see a big, tall tree in the distance. The tree is in Foncha Avenue. That's the fifth street from here. The Post Office is beside the tree.
>
> 10,

Picture 19: John and Mary providing travelling directives to a stranger. Evans (book4):10.

Techniques of intertextuality and intratextuality

Picture illustrations use techniques of intertextuality and intratextuality to highlight certain traditional discourses where notions of wealth, importance and division of labour are on gender lines.

Intertextual presentations of educational materials in pictures 3 and 4, 7 and 8, 9 and 10, 11 and 12, 17 and 18 portray gender discrimination in which the female, on the one hand, is more inclined to do shopping, being a nurse and luggage handler, making and serving coffee, possessing things of perishable nature, domestic chores, incompetence in cycling, while on the other hand, the male is shown to be a high university don of mathematics, a medical doctor, a pilot, a maker of bicycles, owner of pets and animals, and competence in observing traffic regulations while cycling. The juxtaposition of activities of the female to that of the male reveal gender bias which consistently favours the male.

Intratextuality contrasts implicitly events in the same picture like in picture 2 and 19. Picture 2 shows Mrs. Baba apportioning house work to Aissatou and herself and Arouna and Mamadou go out shepherding and paddling. Picture 19 shows John's ability to supply directives to the stranger while Mary in the same picture is incapable. She makes mistakes in giving the directives to find a way.

These intertextual and intratextual pictorial presentations are gender bias, they lack transparency and objectivity.

The implicit messages created by these techniques on gender lines fail to train women and girls to see themselves to be publicly important. The nursery and primary including secondary schools should serve as incubators which mould the girl child with self-esteem.

In certain cases the female is presented as a gift to reward boys who achieved a challenging mission. Evans (book3):37-39

Picture 20

Picture 21

Picture 22

Why should women be shown as a reward to achievers who are boys in picture 22? When did women become objects?

Gender frequency in the three manual series

Frequency counts deal with the relative frequency of occurrence of items and their habitual co-occurrence in different contexts. Let us examine the re-occurrence of **she/he, him/her, his/her** and **brother/sister** in four books of each series *Evans, Champions, Go for English,* in table 2.

Table 2

Gender usage	Evans Cameroon primary English				Total	Ratio of M:F
Books	3	4	5	6		
Male subject (he)	110	192	146	209	657	
Female subject (she)	46	76	65	72	259	5:2
Male genitives (his)	16	82	18	174	290	
Female genitives (her)	16	30	54	19	119	5:2
Brother	11	21	18	10	60	
Sister	2	6	10	40	58	30:29
	Champions in English					
Books	3	4	5	6		
Male object (him)	---	1	4	15	20	
Female object (her)	---	1	4	11	16	10:8
Male genitives (his)	22	23	34	37	116	
Female genitives (her)	19	22	26	36	103	58:51
Brother	3	4	2	4	13	
Sister	2	6	2	4	14	13:14
	Go for English					
Books	3	4	5	6		
Male object (him)	15	41	60	138	254	
Female object (her)	19	18	36	70	143	23:13
Male genitives (his)	80	80	161	201	522	
Female genitives (her)	51	45	70	171	337	3:2
Brother	32	13	23	18	86	
Sister	21	4	10	17	52	5:3

The word **brother** appears 159 times and **sister** 124 times in the twelve books of the three series. This is an indicator that more prominence is given to brother than sister. This is in keeping with the various pronominal occurrences which put male pronouns on the ascendancy.

Key Word in Context Concordance (KWIC)

Gender bias can occur in very subtle ways, discrimination can be identified through linguistic traces as association of meaning which can produce entirely different interpretation of linguistically neutral words.

Go for English book 5 uses the verb **works** with different associations according to their being male and female.

Male   female

Works

Male	female
In the workshop	in the kitchen
As a plane captain	in the house
As a waiter	on the farm
As a cleaner	as a hostess
As a sailor	for long hours on land that belongs to their husbands
Hard at high	school
On the idea	in the field
From dusk to dawn	as a cook
20 hours a day	as a nurse
To organise a concert	as a hairdresser

	At the airport in
a nearby jeweller's shop
	With metal
with animals
	On the family farm
harder than men but
	As a vet
earns less
	On a sugar plantation
for landlords
	With beriberi patients to
furnish the house
	Like war animals as
a servant
	For several months
in cotton fields

as a dressmaker

		Figure 1

The male works as a provider of services or producer of goods while the female works as a
	caretaker or as a nurse as can be gleaned in figure 1.
	Examples in *Go for English* 1ere and 4e are verbs: **wins, makes, writes, invents, have/has (possess)** which are used as follows:

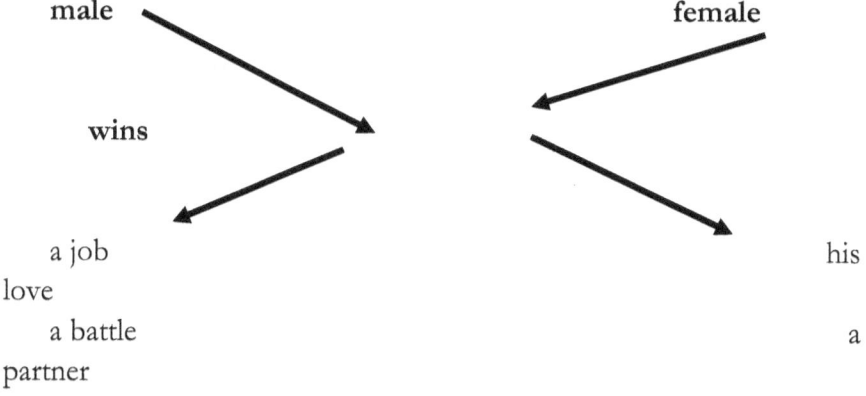

	a job his
love
	a battle a
partner

    a wrestling competition   his favour
    the Tropicana championship   a person she will like to marry
    a lottery
    a scholarship to study   a ticket to travel round the world
    elections
    several international prizes   a gold medal
    prize in the national lottery
    all men's event
    his country's first Olympic medal
    a marathon medal
    a competition
    the sports prize
    the Olympic light weight
    world heavy weight title
    prizes for mathematics
    a race

Figure 2

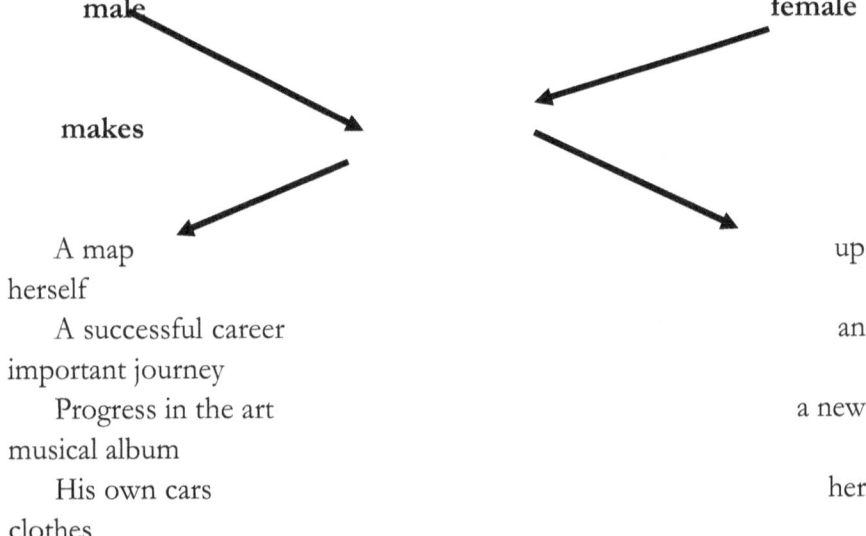

    male   **female**

    makes

    A map   up herself
    A successful career   an important journey
    Progress in the art   a new musical album
    His own cars   her clothes

A piece of	equipment	(modern) women beautiful and attractive
A story to tell the headmaster		silly mistakes
An error in	business	dealings themselves beautiful
The most skilled sandals		a cake
Fun of him		new friends
By craftsmen		no loan to make her business
A general		a cup of tea
Friends		
Some money		
Fabulous swords		
Famous smiths of Kano		
A film		
Paper		
A record		
A welcome speech		
A very good impression		
A new drink		
Logs		
A wooden drum		
A beautiful sculpture		
A plate		
The frame		
The brakes		
The fork		
A name for himself		

Figure 3

The use of the verbs (wins and makes) does not overtly show any bias. But the various objects with which they collocate reveal certain subtle semantic gender bias. It is being insinuated in figure 2 that a man wins a scholarship to study, to improve his knowledge or wins challenging competitions but a woman wins a person she will like to marry. This reflects the independency / dependency dichotomy in our society of man-made world. In the same vein, the collocations of **makes** in relation to man suggest production or paid services while those of the female are mostly insignificant or free. While men make reasonable objects that can be helpful to society like sandals, films, cars, records, papers, women are busy making themselves beautiful and attractive and making silly mistakes with no loans to make their business successful as figure 3 illustrates.

The verbs **writes** and **invents** indicate many activities around men and practically nothing on women as shown on figures 4 and 5

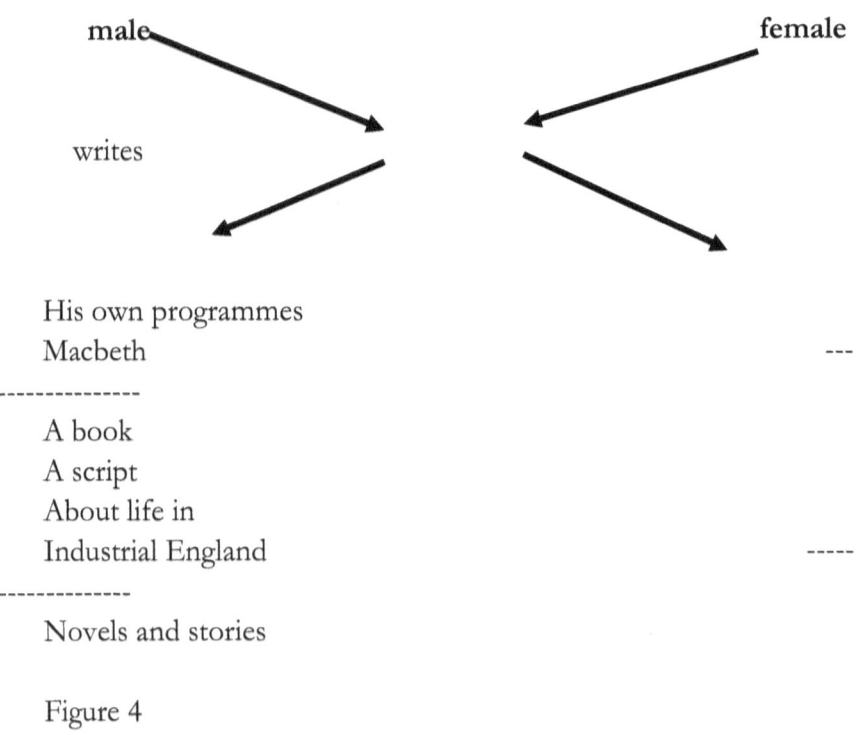

Figure 4

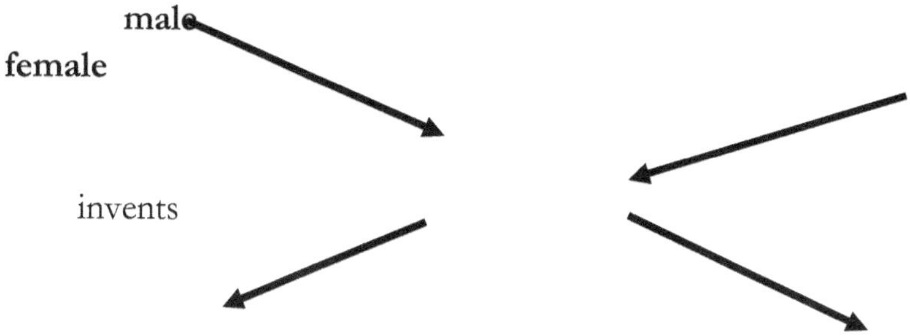

```
        male
female
                invents

    Factory assembly line
    Julian calendar                              ---
------------------
    Negritude
    Bamoun script
    Basket ball in 1891
    A new system of writing
    A system using dots
    Braille alphabet                             ---
------------------
    Arts and science
    The printing press
                Figure 5
```

It is shown in figures 4 and 5 that women have no acumen to write nor the talents to invent or create anything. Such activities are non-existent in their realm of life since there is insinuation that women are only consumers.

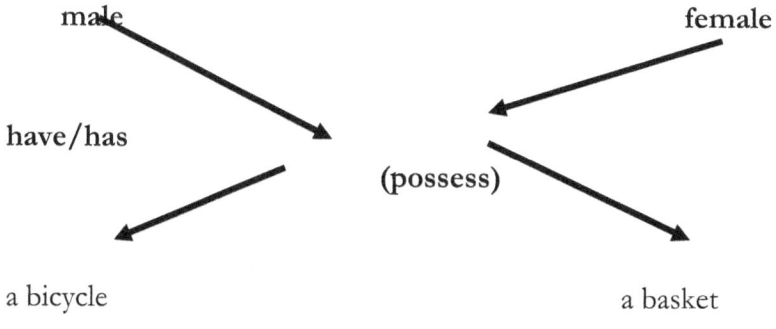

a car	a doll
a kite	a bag
a dog	a cat
a house	many plantains
many hens	many pineapples
many cows	two cassavas
A ball	six eggs
many animals	two pumpkins
mathematics today	one red pepper
history today	four tomatoes

Figure 6

All the associated items with **have/has** in figure 6 show men owning things of great money value while women seem to content themselves with domestic toys, pets and foodstuffs. This is another hidden bias in educational materials which socialise young learners unconsciously.

Closing remarks

The majority of the world's population is women. This is not reflected proportionately in the conception of the English school manuals; whether stories, picture illustrations, title captions and activities in which women and girls appear in low frequency while men and boys appear in their numbers here and there. All these point to the fact that men and boys are the community's focus while women and girls constitute only an appendix.

An educational environment like schools is an enabling place for the formative development of young learners where boys and girls should participate in role play and traditional discourses without regard to sex.

This obliges textbook writers to exercise a critical sense when they present their pedagogic materials to the young learners as they by nature will be receptive to them. Ideas and the gendered division of labour which are well couched in the manuals are unconsciously assimilated by the learners. Male and female characters in the manuals should not confine themselves on gender basis. They should be seen to interact with each other by participating in all activities without strict gender distinction. It looks doctrinaire to assign gender roles in the manuals strictly on the basis of the traditional division of labor where the girl child is for family chores and the boy for outdoor activities which relate to paid and high money value. Discriminatory gender roles and identities should have no room in our classroom activities.

It has been a pedagogic truism that school manuals should seek to reflect local realities which are truly anchored on the environment of the learner. While this sounds a healthy thing to practise it should not be carried out unimaginatively. Names of objects, people and local practices should be a true reflection of the ambient society, but retrograde practices, like gender discrimination, gender division of labour and gender subservience, a practice cherished in the traditional society should find no room in educational materials in the classroom which is a liberating force, not a vitiating one, for the learner par excellence

When it is observed that pedagogic materials encode practices that undermine the healthy growth and fulfilment of the girl child then one begins to discern problems entrenched in the formative process of such young learners. Our educational enterprise should generate and enhance progressive practices and not be seen to perpetuate conservative mores which foster the development and dominance of the boy to the detriment of the girl child. The young learners in the process of acquiring knowledge and skills should find pedagogic materials that are oriented to their linguistic edification without gender bias, so that the classroom should not become a laboratory for gendering the learners

References

Atanga, L.L (2007). 'Challenging traditional practices: a study of modern progressive gendered discourses in the Cameroonian parliament' (manuscript).

Atanga, L.L. (2007). *Gendered Discourses in the Cameroonian Parliament.* PhD thesis. Lancaster. Lancaster University.

Bauer, L, Janet Holmes and Paul Warren (2006). *Language matters.* Basingstoke: Macmillan

Cameron, D.C (1985). *What has gender got to do with sex, language and communication?* London: Routlege and Kegan Paul

Caroll, D and Johanna Kowitz (1990). 'An objective tool for textbook evaluation and selection'. (manuscript) IATEFL conference. Dublin

Coates, J, and Deborah Cameron (eds), (1989). *Women in their speech communities.* London: Longman.

De Bot et al (2005*). Second language acquisition. An advanced Resource book.* London: Longman

Cripwell, K et al.(1992). *Go for English.* 3e, 4e. Edicef: Macmillan

Heward, C and Sheila Bunwaree, (eds), (1999). *Gender, education and development beyond access to empowerment*, London: Zed Books Ltd

Lakoff, R. (1975).*Language and women's place.* New York: Harper and Row

Mbangwana, P. (1996): 'Trends in female names: expression of self-affirmation' *Epasa Moto* no.11, pp 75-80

Mineduc (1999) *Champions in English.* bks SIL, CP, CE1, CE2, CM1, CM2

Morton (2000) In: Ellis, R. and Barkhuizen (2005). *Analysing learner language.* London : OUP.

Ndangam,A and David Weir.(2000): *Evans Cameroon primary English.* bks 3,4,5. London: Evans Brothers Ltd.

Spender, D. (1980): *Man-made language*, London: Routlege and Kegan Paul

Sunderland, J. (1994): *Exploring gender, questions and implications for English language education.* London: Prentice Hall International Ltd

Sunderland, J. (2004) *Gendered Discourses. Basingstoke: Palgrave*

Whorf, B.L. (1956): *Language, thought and reality.* Cambridge: Mass. MIT Press.

6

Genre Et Langage Dans L'espace Partisan Camerounais: La Promotion De La Femme Dans Les Productions Symboliques De L'UNC Au RDPC

Caroline Ngamchara Mbouemboue
Université De Dschang

Introduction

En proclamant l'universalisme politique depuis sa première constitution (Sindjoun & Owona Nguni, 2000), l'Etat camerounais donne l'impression d'avoir très tôt voulu se constituer en terrain favorable à l'épanouissement social, économique, mais surtout politique des *« minorités sociologiques »* (Balandier, 1971). Et l'Union camerounaise (UC) qui deviendra son bras politique à l'ère monolithique, puis parti au pouvoir depuis le retour au multipartisme brille déjà à ses origines par un discours volontariste suivi de mesures *«en faveur »* de certaines de ces *« minorités sociologiques »*, les femmes en l'occurrence (Ahidjo, 1964 ; Bayart, 1985).

Jusqu'en début des années 1980 se pose avec acuité la question de l'opérationnalité de ces mesures, et de l'identité de leurs véritables bénéficiaires. La branche féminine en particulier (OFUNC)[7] poursuivait apparemment des objectifs contradictoires : loin de concourir à la politisation de ses recrues, elle aurait plutôt contribué à les mobiliser et à les conforter dans la position de *« cadettes sociales »* qui faisait d'elles l'un des supports du projet hégémonique du président Ahidjo (Bayart, 1985 ; Eteki Otabela, 1987 ; Konda, 2005).

Puis, de nombreuses voix - féminines surtout - se sont élevées contre cette situation (Sindjoun & Owona op. cit.). Les réformes entreprises dans ce parti depuis le congrès des 21 au 24 avril 1985 ont donné lieu à d'autres mesures *« en faveur des femmes »*. Non seulement

---

[7] La principale mesure est précisément celle dont la plupart d'observateurs doutent de la capacité à assurer l'intégration et l'empouvoirement politiques des femmes (Union interparlementaire, 1989 :66-68).

l'OFRDPC a formellement changé de structure et de fonction, mais les militantes ont aussi bénéficié de mesures à même de booster leur empouvoirement (voir par exemple la circulaire n° 02/RDPC/PN du 25 avril 2007). Mais ces mesures s'inscrivent-elles dans une dynamique de reconfiguration de l'ordre sexuel du parti?

Une sociologie de la littérature produite dans et pour le fonctionnement de ce parti permet de s'interroger sur l'évolution ambiante des attitudes de genre. Car de nombreuses études retrouvent dans les productions symboliques des organisations, des éléments permettant d'en appréhender l'ordre sexuel (Gilligan, 1982 ; Wodak, 2009), ordre que ces productions contribuent aussi à construire et à consolider (Talbot, 1998 ; Eckert & McConnel-Ginet, 2003).

Et de toutes les productions symboliques des partis, les textes de base sont d'une importance capitale : ils présentent la plate-forme qui est à la base de l'entreprise politique (la charte) tout comme les éléments qui contribuent de façon réelle mais surtout symbolique à créer une dynamique collective au sein des militants (sceaux, sigles, etc.), organisent les activités de militantisme (règlement intérieur), etc. Ainsi, ils permettent d'appréhender le *« capital partisan objectivé »* (Offerlé, 2002 :16). Et les textes de base qui permettent de rendre compte des reformes antérieures et postérieures au *« congrès du renouveau »* (RDPC, 1986) sont d'une part ceux qui précèdent le congrès de Bamenda et d'autre part ceux qui sont en vigueur en cette fin des années 2000.

Ces textes sont soumis à l'analyse de l'énonciation qui permet de reconstituer des attitudes latentes ou refoulées (Bardin, 2003 ; Guillaumin, 1972). Et cette lecture en profondeur des textes passe par une première analyse catégorielle attentive à la forme (genre) lexicale ou thématique des énoncés qui réglementent la vie militante. Cette analyse thématique et lexicale permet d'abord de voir comment la fréquence ou l'absence de certains énoncés apparaît comme la face émergée d'un milieu partisan dominé par des référentiels masculins (1), lesquels référentiels se matérialisent dans une ségrégation de l'espace partisan consacrée par un certain ordre des occurrences (2) ce qui pose plus fondamentalement la question de la construction du problème féminin et de ses solutions (3).

Distribution des substantifs masculins et féminins dans les chartes : de l'invisibilité du féminin aux référentiels patriarcaux du milieu partisan

La charte qui peut être définie comme un corps de lois constitutionnelles d'une organisation fournit des éléments relatifs aux nécessaires repères idéels qui guident l'action collective (Bréchon, 1999). Elle permet ainsi de saisir le cadre référentiel de base d'une organisation. En ce sens, l'hégémonie des substantifs masculins dans les chartes de l'UNC puis du RDPC se présente comme un indicateur d'un milieu partisan encore dominé par une idéologie phallocratique.

De l'invisibilité du féminin dans la charte de l'UNC

Sur le plan lexical, le déséquilibre en faveur des substantifs masculins est d'abord manifeste dans l'évocation de *« l'humanité »*. Dans tout le texte, le morphème *« femme »* n'apparaît qu'une seule fois, quand il devient incontournable (il est question des organismes annexes, des mouvements des jeunes et des femmes, thèse N°12, p.52). En revanche, chaque fois qu'il est question de l'humanité apparaissent des substantifs qui, appliqués ou non aux deux sexes, donnent l'impression de ne prendre que le *« sexe fort »* en considération. Il est ainsi question de *« Déclaration Universelle des droits de l'homme »*[8] (thèse N°9, p.50), de « *l'épanouissement de l'homme Camerounais** » (Thèse N°27, p.58)... Pour ce qui est du développement économique, social et culturel, c'est, *« en dernière analyse, l'homme qui en est le catalyseur »* (titre N°24, p.56), lequel homme est pour la société *« le capital le plus précieux »* (thèse N°25, p56), etc.

Mais cette primauté du masculin est aussi la règle pour tous les autres substantifs qui renvoient à l'espace politique, le parti et même la société en général. Ainsi, l'indépendance consistera à œuvrer pour l'épanouissement des *« habitants »* (thèse N°2, p.48), l'Etat camerounais donnera au peuple la possibilité de participer *« au choix de ses dirigeants »* (thèse N°9, p.50); par ailleurs le parti groupera *« tous les citoyens camerounais sans exclusive »* (thèse 12, p.52), citoyens dont l'activité partisane sera régulée par la rubrique *« Droits et devoirs du militant »*.

---

[8] Même s'il est d'usage de le libeller comme il suit : *Déclaration universelle des droits de l'Homme.* * (sic)

Qu'il s'agisse ou non de lapsus, la forme de ces substantifs tend à faire des hommes les cibles exclusives de ces textes. Il est vrai qu'en français tous les substantifs sont dotés d'un genre motivé ou non (Wagner et Pinchon, 1991) et que ces usages ne font d'une certaine façon qu'obéir aux règles régissant la flexion nominale dans cette langue, règles qui font du masculin le neutre. Mais justement, sous des pressions diverses, la configuration du neutre n'a pas cessé de subir des modifications : ainsi est-il de plus en plus d'usage de faire appel aux majuscules dans certaines circonstances (Homme), d'achever les morphèmes qui en prennent au féminin par un « e » entre parenthèse : citoyen(e), habitant(e)s, militant(e), etc. Car de nombreux auteurs sont revenus sur le caractère illusoire de ce neutre au masculin qui n'en exprime pas moins un certain ordre sexuel des sociétés qui de façon implicite constituent le masculin en une norme, ou en l'*« essentiel »*, faisant du féminin l'*« inessentiel »* (De Beauvoir, 1999). Cet ordre est d'ailleurs encore largement en vigueur au Cameroun (UNICEF, 1997 ; *Profil femme et développement au Cameroun*, 1996).

Des édulcorations marginales dans la charte du RDPC

La charte du RDPC qui a globalement gardé les mêmes articulations que celle de l'UNC n'apporte que des changements marginaux aux énoncés susmentionnés.

Pour ce qui est des substantifs, s'il est enfin question des « *Droits de l'Homme »* (thèse 9, p.138) et qu'apparaissent d'autres expressions destinées en apparence à limiter le masculin telles que *« bien-être des Camerounais »* (RDPC, Thèse 24, p.146), *« l'Homme camerounais »* (thèse 25, p.146), ces changements ne semblent pas systématiques : ils sont souvent suivis des substantifs *« neutres au masculin »* qui se sont paradoxalement multipliés. Dans les passages qui constituent des amendements à la charte précédente, il est question que le parti accorde une importance particulière « *à la formation des hommes notamment dans les domaines scientifiques et techniques »* (thèse 4, p146), et en conclusion fasse appel à *« tous les citoyens conscients de leurs responsabilités à l'égard de leur pays à se rassembler …»* (thèse 31, p150), etc.

Dans tous les cas l'expression d'une phallocratie

Mais cette invisibilité des substantifs féminins est loin de n'être qu'un jeu de mots. Les chartes de l'UNC puis du RDPC semblent reposer largement sur des idéologies classiques du pouvoir, de l'Etat, du peuple, de la souveraineté ; celles d'Aristote, mais surtout de Machiavel ou de Jean Bodin réputées pour leur caractère patriarcal (Bethke Elshtain, 1941 ; Optiz, 1997 ; Le Bras-Chopard & Mossuz-Lavau, 1997). Ces visions du politique et de son cadre d'exercice célébrant largement des valeurs viriles qui sont encore celles de la république camerounaise (Sindjoun & Owona Nguini, op. cit.) semblent se configurer depuis le parti au pouvoir.

Pour ce qui est de l'Etat par exemple, des quatre visages qui lui sont reconnus par Pierre Rosanvalon (Sciences humaines, 2002 :145), c'est surtout la fonction régalienne (celle qui correspond le plus aux attributs de la masculinité) qui est décrite, ce qui a une forme d'incidence sur la description qui est faite du gouvernement. Ainsi, dans les deux chartes, l'Etat sera caractérisé par la *« force matérielle »* afin d'assurer *« l'exécution de ses décisions »* (RDPC, thèse7, p138) ; et le régime présidentiel est l'option qui permet de *« renforcer l'autorité de l'Etat en vue de parvenir rapidement à l'intégration nationale »* (thèse N°10, p.138).

Ainsi, l'invisibilité des substantifs féminins semble n'être que la face émergée d'un univers politique configuré à partir de référentiels politiques quelques peu virils. Ces référentiels de base trouvent encore des lieux d'illustration dans les mécanismes d'organisation des activités et de structuration de l'espace partisan.

Distribution du masculin et du féminin dans les statuts et règlements intérieurs

Les statuts qui présentent partiellement les *« ressources collectives partisanes »* (Offerlé 2002 :36) et les règlements intérieurs centrés sur les éléments qui pour P. Bernoux, sont les principaux traits de l'organisation à savoir la division des tâches, la distribution des rôles, le système d'autorité, le système de communication, le système de contribution rétribution (Bernoux , 1985), sont des données majeures pour l'intelligibilité des mécanismes de fonctionnement d'un parti. Si les conduites individuelles et collectives ne sont pas des décalques de ces textes, elles s'en inspirent largement. C'est pour cela que le mode de dissémination des substantifs masculins et féminins ici peut être un indicateur des trajectoires militantes de l'un et l'autre sexe.

De la dissémination du masculin et du féminin à la ségrégation sexuelle de l'espace partisan dans les statuts et le règlement intérieur de l'UNC

Si l'on constate encore le primat des énoncés *« neutres au masculin »* dans ce parti qui se propose consolider l' *« égalité de tous devant la loi »*, lutter pour *« le bien être de tous »* (UNC, art. 2, p.10), parti dont est membre *« tout camerounais* âgé de ... » (art. 6, p.12) et dans lequel *« nul ne peut être admis [...] s'il est membre d'un autre parti ... »* (art. 8, p.12) au lieu par exemple des usages plus neutres comme *« tous et toutes »*, *« tout(e) »*, *« il(elle) »*, etc. ; plus intéressante est cette ségrégation de l'espace partisan consacrée par la distribution de ces énoncés dans les divers tâches, rôles, positions d'autorité, etc.. Les organes mixtes que sont l'UNC et l'OJUNC verront systématiquement les énoncés de leurs postes et fonctions déclinés dans ce « neutre au masculin ».

Pour ce qui est de l'UNC, si l'usage des chiffres arabes laisse planer un doute sur le genre de certains postes, il s'ensuit toujours un retour au masculin. Ainsi la cellule qui est constituée d'une part de *« 1 Responsable, 1 Secrétaire [...], 1 Commissaire à la jeunesse, 1 Commissaire à l'OFUNC »* compte aussi en son sein *« 2 Délégués à l'éducation et à la propagande, 1 trésorier »* (art.15, p.46) ; ce qui donne finalement des allures de *« un »* au chiffre précédent les autres postes. Au niveau de la section, le doute n'a plus de place car l'on a à faire à des substantifs qui changent au féminin *« 1 Président, 2 Vice-Présidents*, 5 Délégués..., 1 Trésorier »* ou que les substantifs invariables sont accompagnés d'autres qui en précisent le genre (*« 1 Secrétaire »*, mais *« 2 Secrétaires- adjoints »*). Il en est ainsi jusqu'au sommet du parti. Les titres des postes et des fonctions vont présenter la même configuration pour l'OJUNC.

Ces énoncés des postes et des fonctions reviendront systématiquement au féminin dans l'OFUNC, de la cellule à la section. Pour ce qui est de la cellule, le doute qui plane sur *« 1 Responsable »*, *« 1 Secrétaire »* sera rattrapé par *« 1 conseillère »* ; et au niveau de la section, celui qui plane sur *« 1 Secrétaire »*, *« 2 Commissaires au compte »* sera rattrapé par *« 1 Présidente, 2 Vice-Présidentes* ...1 Secrétaire Adjointe* ... »* (art.31, pp.26-28). Mais cet usage du féminin reste limité. Dans les organes centraux de l'OFUNC, la place est de nouveau faite au *« neutre masculin »*, surtout pour ceux des membres qui viennent de l'organe central du parti.

Or, de nombreuses études montrent que le genre des titres et des fonctions n'est pas anodin. De façon explicite ou implicite, il renvoie aux rôles sociaux conférés à l'un ou l'autre sexe en contexte d'action organisé, rôles qu'ils contribuent aussi à perpétrer (Barbry, 2000 ; Houdebine-Gravaud, 1999). C'est pour cela que dans de nombreux pays d'expression française, la féminisation de la langue a d'abord commencé par les titres et les fonctions (ibid.). Les usages sélectifs du masculin et du féminin dans les titres et les fonctions cessent ainsi d'être anodins. Ils contribuent à remettre en question la mixité dans l'UNC et l'OJUNC surtout qu'ils donnent l'impression de légitimer une structuration l'espace partisan qui confine les femmes dans de véritables *« ghettos »* identitaires (Lamizet, 2002 :208).

De la ségrégation de l'espace partisan au même militantisme de seconde zone pour les femmes dans le RDPC

Les statuts et le règlement intérieur du RDPC de 1996 reprennent en substance la même configuration des énoncés masculins et féminins. Ici encore, le masculin reste le neutre pour ce qui est des substantifs: Dans les ajouts aux textes antérieurs, il est question d' *« un adhérent »*, du *« Président »*, du *« Trésorier »* des *« électeurs »* (art.7, p.68), des *« Présidents de cellules »* (art.26, p.78), etc. Le féminin n'apparaîtra une fois de plus que lorsqu'il est question de l'organe spécialisé *« les militantes et les militants des Organisations Spécialisées du parti (OJRDPC et OFRDPC) »*. Les titres et les fonctions sont encore systématiquement déclinés au masculin pour le RDPC et l'OJRDPC ; et à l'OFRDPC, ils font l'objet d'une féminisation sélective qui donne des allures masculines à la tutelle de l'organe central du parti.

Mais il est un changement qui fait parler de lui, c'est le passage de la branche féminine d'*« organe annexe »* à *« organe spécialisé »*. Et pourtant, ce changement ne s'accompagne pas d'un nouveau vocabulaire pour cet espace partisan. L'OFUNC était *« apolitique »* et *« sous tutelle »* avait pour but la *« mobilisation des femmes [...] en vue de l'accomplissement des œuvres sociales du parti »* avec pour commissions *« Affaires sociales et culturelles, Arts ménagers, Fêtes et sports »* (titre IV, pp.24-32). Ces fonctions et attributs font qu'un militantisme exclusif dans cette branche éloigne des instances de pouvoir interne et des postes électifs, et même des affaires politiques ; ce qui rapproche l'espace partisan des sociétés traditionnelle (Atanga, 2007 ; Cameron 2006**)**. Les femmes perdent ainsi leur caractère de militantes à part entière pour se comporter en adjuvantes des militants de l'organe central. L'expression « *œuvres sociales du parti* » donne l'impression qu'elles ne font pas réellement partie de ces espaces.

Depuis que l'OFRDPC est devenue « *organe spécialisé* » chargée d'intégrer les femmes dans tous les domaines de la vie nationale, ses recrues n'en sont pas moins conçues comme des adjuvantes du parti. Il est encore question de « *mobilisation des femmes camerounaises en vue de leur conscientisation et de leur pleine participation à la poursuite et à la réalisation des objectifs du parti* » (art. 47, p.34). En plus, c'est encore un organe « *sous tutelle* » et cette tutelle donne lieu à un retour du neutre au masculin (ou au retour des hommes ?). En effet, si de la cellule à la section l'OFRDPC est dirigée par des femmes, son Bureau national comporte en plus des 41 membres élus par le Conseil national désignés par des substantifs féminins, « *10 membres désignés par la présidence du Bureau National* [sous-entendu du RDPC] » en plus de « *4 membres de droit : le secrétaire à l'organisation, le secrétaire aux organisations spécialisées du Comité Central et leurs adjoints* » (article 68, p44).

Dans leur expression, les statuts et les règlements intérieurs de l'UNC puis du RDPC semblent bien loin de la neutralité dans la façon dont ils désignent les personnes qui y militent, dont ils organisent les instances dirigeantes, définissent les attributs des postes de responsabilité ; dans la façon dont ils compartimentent l'univers partisan. Partant de ces considérations, quelle lecture peut-on faire du processus de féminisation de cette organisation ?

Du langage phallocentrique à la remise en question de la féminisation du parti

Un survol de la version anglaise des textes soumis à l'analyse permettrait d'évacuer partiellement ces expressions sexistes qui sont pour une bonne part des avatars d'une langue française qui fait l'objet d'un ancrage particulièrement profond dans le genre.

Des résistances linguistiques

Certaines expressions du sexisme qui ont été mises en évidence sont d'abord structurelles à une langue française dont l'ancrage profond dans le genre ne laisse par exemple pas de place au véritable neutre comme c'est le cas pour des langues comme l'anglais, l'Allemand, l'Arabe (Garbry, 2000 ; Trudgill, 2000). De plus, le processus de féminisation de la langue française commencé depuis la fin des années 1970 au Québec, puis en France, et dans d'autres pays comme la Suisse ou la Belgique - processus dont l'UNESCO a fait un de ses objets de bataille[9]- tarde réellement à devenir une priorité dans les pays francophones d'Afrique où la réappropriation de la langue se manifeste davantage par des innovations lexicales (Depecker, 1990) que grammaticales.

Ces résistances sont aussi nécessairement imputables aux concepteurs et rédacteurs de ces textes qui n'ont pas une sensibilité au genre qui leur permette de limiter le masculin par l'usage des termes plus neutres (remplacer par exemple *« homme »* par *« Homme »* ou *« personne »*) ou l'usage des déclinaisons pour les titres et les fonctions (le /la Président(e), le/la Secrétaire, etc.). Mais au-delà, le langage sexiste relevé reflète, quand il ne construit pas des blocages au processus de recomposition des rapports sociaux de sexe dans ce part où la question féminine ne semble pas avoir souvent fait l'objet d'une problématisation systématique.

Le défaut de construction du problème féminin

Mais la fréquence de l'occurrence du masculin, la répartition des substantifs des deux genres semblent poser des problèmes plus structurels à ces textes et partant à ce parti politique : le défaut de problématisation de la question féminine. L'on semble en effet faire une impasse totale sur ce problème identitaire tout en prétendant y apporter des solutions.

Ainsi, dans la charte de l'UNC, la nation sera cette collectivité humaine qui ne dépasse que « *les particularismes ethniques, religieux et linguistiques* » (thèse N°4, p.48). Le parti qui se propose de concourir à l'émergence de cette nation *« condamne énergiquement le tribalisme et toutes autres divisions politiques »* (thèse N°14, p.22). Il mènera même

---

[9] Ce processus à donné lieu à de nombreux guides pour la féminisation du langage : Pour le Canada, H. Dumas, *Pour un genre à part entière : guide pour la réduction des textes sexistes*, Gouvernement du Québec, Ministère de l'éducation, 1988 ; M. Biron et al., *Au féminin : guide de la féminisation des titres des fonctions et des textes*, Gouvernement du Québec, Office de la langue française 1991 ; UNESCO, Guidelines on Gender Neutral Language, 1999.

auparavant une bataille préventive afin que ne se cristallisent des « *classes sociales hostiles* » (thèse N°12 :52) alors que les clivages sociaux de sexe qui existent déjà ne font l'objet d'aucune mention explicite.

La charte du RDPC qui date de plusieurs décennies reste une copie conforme de celle de l'UNC. Le sexisme ne figure pas de façon explicite parmi les clivages présentés comme des menaces à la cohésion sociale. Le Cameroun n'est divers que dans sa structure ethnique, linguistique, religieuse et culturelle (thèse N°5 : p136), même si le parti condamne « *toutes sortes de discriminations* » (thèse N°14, p.140).

Cette invisibilité du problème féminin se veut aussi la règle dans les règlements intérieurs. Si les dispositions générales du règlement de l'UNC ne connaissent que la loi de la majorité dans les processus décisionnels, l'on note certes une avancée dans le RDPC où il est question de respect des droits des minorités même si ce respect n'empêche pas la soumission de cette minorité à la majorité (art.2, p.64). Mais dans tous les cas, l'apparition du terme *« minorité »* ici ne s'accompagne pas d'une spécification de son contenu et il est difficile de ne pas en faire un avatar des stratégies de constitutionnalisation des conflits ethniques et sociolinguistiques qui secouent le Cameroun depuis la fin des années 1980 (Sindjoun, 1999).

La féminisation en question

Les expressions sexistes relevées ont tendance à perpétrer une ségrégation sexuelle non plus théorique mais pratique de l'espace partisan, remettant en cause l'intention d'intégration politique des femmes. Le système d'autorité de l'organe central se constitue ainsi en la chasse gardée des hommes comme le traduit d'ailleurs la façon dont est souvent décliné le titre des femmes à ces postes : certaines continuent à *être* « *Mme le Président de section RDPC* » alors que du côté de la branche féminine il a toujours été question de « *Mme la Présidente de section OFRDPC* ». Ces usages montrent que dans l'imaginaire collectif, les accessions féminines à ces postes ne sont que des exceptions qui confirment une certaines règle.

Et plus fondamentalement, l'absence d'allusions explicites aux particularismes sexuels dans les textes de base ne laisse-t-elle pas planer un doute sur les efforts pour construire ce problème dans ce parti surtout que d'autres textes essentiels comme le support doctrinal (Biya, 1987) n'en font pas une priorité ? Par ailleurs, si les réformes entreprises depuis 1985 ont donné lieu à une abondante littérature, la plupart d'analystes qui reviennent sur les réformes idéologiques, les recompositions des bases ethniques et générationnelles du parti ne problématisent pas réellement les changements en termes de genre (Mono Ndjana, 1992 ; Oyono, 1996 ; Mbassi, 2004).

Et si les efforts pour construire le problème sexuel restent limités, un parti peut-il engager un véritable processus d'institutionnalisation du féminisme en son sein ? Les contradictions des textes de base qui expriment des efforts pour un encadrement particulier des femmes dans un langage phallocentrique, la présentation des mécanismes de fonctionnement du RDPC qui atteste encore de ce masculin qui se cache sous la mixité dans l'espace partisan (Gaspard, 1997) ; et plus globalement la branche féminine qui change de configuration sans changer de vocabulaire, montrent le caractère toujours à construire de la promotion féminine au sein du RDPC.

Conclusion

Cette contribution se proposait de partir des expressions du sexisme dans le langage des textes de base de l'UNC puis du RDPC pour apporter des éléments permettant d'apprécier globalement le processus de féminisation en cours dans ce parti depuis les années 1960. La charte, les statuts et le règlement intérieur de l'UNC ont révélé une expression caractérisée par une invisibilité totale du féminin, des allusions à des rôles sexuels stéréotypés, puis une absence d'effort visant à construire le problème de genre dans cette organisation. Ces données qui ne sont que partiellement imputables à une langue française caractérisée par un ancrage particulièrement profond dans le genre se sont aussi voulues révélatrices de défaillances dans le processus de promotion féminine alors en cours.

Si l'avènement du RDPC s'est traduite par les réformes des bases idéologiques, programmatiques et autres du parti, celles des reformes qui touchent le complexe des relations humaines (et surtout les relations de genre) n'ont pas forcément été profondes si l'on en juge par le langage des textes de base qui se démarque encore difficilement des textes précédents, tout comme tout le vocabulaire dans lequel s'exprime l'être des femmes dans ce parti. C'est pourquoi des décennies de mesures en *« faveur des femmes »* ne les empêchent pas de peiner à s'intégrer dans l'espace politique en général (Kassea, 2004) et à faire entendre leur voix dans les instances décisionnelles (Atanga, 2007).

La féminisation d'une organisation cesse alors d'être le produit d'une simple multiplication de mesures. Elle devient une dynamique d'ensemble dans laquelle se construit un problème, se définissent des politiques, le tout transmis dans un langage qui reflète les évolutions en cours ou recherchées.

Références

Ahidjo, A., (1964). *Contribution à la construction nationale*, Paris : Présence africaine.

Atanga, L. L. (2007). *Gendered Discourses in the Cameroonian Parliament*, Thèse de Doctorat PHD, Lancaster: Université de Lancaster

Bardin, L. (2003). « *L'analyse de contenu et de la forme des communications* », S. Moscovici & F. Buschini (dir.), *Les méthodes des sciences sociales*, Paris: PUF, pp.243-270.

Bayart, J.-F., (1985). *L'Etat au Cameroun*, Paris: Presses de la FNSP.

Beauvoir, S. de (1999). *Le deuxième sexe*, Paris: Folio & Gallimard.

Bernoux, P. (1985). *La sociologie des organisations*, Paris: Seuil.

Bethke Alshtain. (1944). *Public Man, Private Woman: Women in Social and Political Thought*, Princeton: Princeton University Press.

Biya, P. (1987). *Pour le libéralisme communautaire*, Paris: Favre ABC.

Bourdieu, P. (1982). *Leçon sur la leçon*, Paris: Minuit.

(1998). *La domination masculine*, Paris: Seuil.

Bréchon, (1999). *Les partis politiques*, Paris: Montchrestien.

Depecker, L. (1990). *Les mots de la francophonie*, Paris, Belin.

Eckert, P. and McConnel-Ginet, S (2003). *Language and Gender*, Cambridge: Cambridge University Press.

Etéki-Otabela, M.-L. (1987). *Misère et grandeur de la démocratie au Cameroun*, Paris: L'Harmattan.

Gardes-Tamine, J. (2002). *La grammaire. 1- Phonologie, morphologie, lexicologie*, Paris: Armand Colin.

Gaspard, F. (1997). « Système politique et rareté des femmes élues : une spécificité française ? », *Les femmes et la politique*, A. Le Bras-Chopard et J. Mossuz-Lavau (dir.), Paris: L'Harmattan, pp98-110.

Gilligan, C., (1982). *In a Different Voice: Psychological Theory of Women's Development*, Cambridge: Harvard University Press.

Guillaumin, C. (1972). *L'idéologie raciste, genèse et langage actuel*, Paris: Mouton.

Houdebine-Gravaud, A.-M., (1999). « La féminisation des noms de métiers », *Un siècle d'antiféminisme*, Christine Bard (dir.), Paris: Fayard, pp431-448.

Lamizet, B. (2002). *Politique et identité*, Lyon: PUL.

Le Bras-Chopard, A & Mossuz-Lavau, J. (dir.), (1997). *Les femmes et la politique*, Paris: L'Harmattan.

Mbassi, L. (2004). *Le temps de la réforme*, Yaoundé : eds. Ulrich.

Mono Ndjana, H. (1992). *La mutation : essai sur le changement politique au Cameroun*, Yaoundé : Ed. du Carrefour.

Offerlé, M. (ed.) (2002). *Les partis politiques*, Paris: PUF.

Optitz, C., (1997). *« Souveraineté et subordination des femmes chez Luther, Calvin, Bodin »*, *Encyclopédie politique et historique des femmes*, C. Faure (dir.), Paris: PUF, pp.31-47.

Oyono, D. (1996). *Un parcours vital : essai sur le renouveau camerounais*, Yaoundé: Edi'Action.

Ambassade des Pays-bas, (1996). *Profil femme et développement au Cameroun*, Yaoundé

RDPC, (1986). *Le congrès du renouveau*, Yaoundé.

Le Pouvoir : des rapports individuels aux relations internationales, Sciences humaines éditions, 2002.

Sindjoun, L., dir, (1999). *La révolution passive au Cameroun : Etat, société et changement*, Dakar: CODESRIA.

Sindjoun, L. & Owona Nguini, M. E., (2000). *« Egalité oblige! Sens et puissance dans les politiques de la femme et les régimes de genre »*, *La biographie sociale du sexe*, L. Sindjoun (dir.), Paris: Karthala & CODESRIA, pp.13-77.

Talbot, M. (1998). *Language and Gender: An Introduction*, Cambridge: Polity Press.

Textes de base de l'Union nationale camerounaise, édition 1980.

Textes de base du Rassemblement démocratique du peuple camerounais, édition 1999.

Trudgill, P. (2000). *Sociolinguistics, An Introduction to Language and Society*, London: Penguin Books.

UNICEF- Cameroun (1997). *Enfants et femmes du Cameroun : analyse de la situation.*

Union interparlementaire, (1989). *Politique : les femmes témoignent,* Série « Rapports &documents », N°36.

Wagner, R. L. et Pinchon, J. (1991). *Grammaire du français classique et moderne,* Paris: Hachette.

Wodak, R. and Meyer, M. (2009). *'Critical discourse analysis: history, agenda, theory and methodology.'* In Wodak, R. and Meyer, M. (eds.), *Methods of Critical Discourse Analysis* (2nd edition), London: Sage.

7

Representation of Gender in Billboard and Poster Adverts of Brewery Products in Cameroon

Canisia Fontem, Lilian Lem Atanga, Jean-Benoît Tsofack
Faculty of Letters and Human Sciences, University Of Dschang, Dschang, Cameroon

Introduction

We are surrounded every day in our lives by adverts. In Cameroon as elsewhere, producers use advertisements to increase their sales and profitability. Gender stereotypes are often linked intentionally or unconsciously with advertising by many manufacturers. Though an extensive literature exist on how gender portrayals in adverts mirror gender roles in society, little of this research has been carried out in Africa especially in Cameroon. The brewery industry is one of such that presents and represents the advertisements of its products using men and women who are the real consumers of these products. The representations and construction of gender on the different products and types is sometimes very binary. As Horsely (2007) observes, these portrayals are a reflection and representation of the societal ideologies or constructs that mirror gender roles in the particular society

The brewery industries are the main actors in the agro industries in Cameroon (MINEFI–DGTPE, 2007). Being in a competitive market in Cameroon as well as the Central African Sub Region, these industries usually sell their products through diverse forms of advertisements amongst them billboards and posters. The objective of this study is to assess the gender representations in billboard and poster adverts of brewery products in Cameroon.

The paper seeks to answer the following research questions:

1. How is gender discursively represented on billboards in Cameroon?

2. Are males and females are equally represented in the adverts of brewery products (alcoholic and soft drinks);

3. How is agency represented in the adverts?

4. Does the representation of gender on billboards reflect societal ideologies and stereotypes?

Methodology

Data selection and collection

The data constitutes billboard and poster adverts of three brewery companies in Cameroon: *Société Anonyme des Brasseries du Cameroun* (SABC), *Union des Brasseries du Cameroun* (UCB), and Guinness Cameroon Société Anonyme (GCSA). Billboards and poster adverts were collected in five of the ten regions of Cameroon (Southwest, Northwest, West, Littoral and Centre). This collection took one month, from the 15 March to 15 April 2009. Although data was collected from only 5 regions of the country, the same adverts reappeared in these regions and are used all over the country. In each region, bill boards were observed along the major highways and streets while wall posters were collected from bars. Each billboard and poster advert was photographed with a digital camera and incorporated into a word file. Printed photos were then assembled and used for numerical analyses of the adverts.

Data analysis

Quantitative analysis of advertisements was focused on the number of adverts that represented a particular theme in the study on various forms of representation (Smith 1994, and Goffman 1976). The numerical representation of gender in brewery product types, number and percentage of male and female representations in the adverts of alcoholic and soft drinks and the number of male and female portrayal of the adverts per drink type were recorded. A quantitative assessment of the numbers of any of these items would give a relative indication of the social constructions present in the advertising (Frith, 1998).

After examining the prevalence of the different gendered discourses, a qualitatively analysis is carried out using critical discourse analysis (Wodak and Meyer). Critical discourse analyses sees language as a social practice (Fairclough 1992). The adverts of the brewery products are designed based on societal stereotypes or ideologies (van Dijk 1998, Thompson 1990, Volosinov 1973). Gendered discourses are identified which present the different representations of males and females in the adverts.

Following Goffman (1976) the data was first examined using the following procedure: Each advert was coded or considered to be either male or female dominant or fore-grounded based on the model that played the most active, independent role. Contrarily, an advert was considered to be male or female backgrounded based on the model that played the most passive, dependent or secondary role. Licenced withdrawal was considered when a model was seemed to be drifting off, gazing away from the camera, engaging the viewer with a seductive eye or a sexually seductive look. Moreover, characters were also identified for decorative or sex appeal poses, whereby the presence of a physically attractive and sexy male or female model was unrelated to the advertised product. The focus was on their body rather than the product; thus as sex object. Consequently adverts were rated for a sight to be gazed upon, an object of another person's gaze or nudity and erotic content portrayal. Adverts were also coded for other themes, such as prizes to be won and sportive portrayals.

Discourse analyses examined how a majority of adverts stressed specific visions of society. From the description of the adverts, we came up with various gendered discourses used in the advertisement media in general and of the brewery products in Cameroon in particular. Gender in the brewery adverts were analysed mostly in their preconceived notion because they are a reflection of the Cameroonian society (cultural construct). All these were meant to examine gender relations in Cameroon which seem to be taking a post-modern turn, thus the subversive and progressive roles of models were also scrutinised.

2.1.1   Consequently, discursive analyses were carried out to bring out the construction of gender through the quantitative scrutiny of the various communication found in the adverts, such as number of different discourses found in the adverts, portrayal of active/dominant role themes in the adverts of brewery products, representations of secondary role themes in the adverts, portrayal of sexual themes and other roles in the adverts.

Structure of the brewery industry in Cameroon

Brewery products found during the study are produced by three major companies in Cameroon. The three companies employed more than 3900 salaried workers and produced more alcoholic than non alcoholic drinks

Proportion of gendered adverts

Bill boards were observed on the major highways and in some cities in Cameroon while posters were observed both in urban and rural areas. On the whole 16 different brewery billboards adverts were encountered along the main roads pertaining to all the companies sampled. 37.5 % had images of females and males and the remaining.

Of the 90 different poster adverts observed during the study, 58.9 %) have human images. Consequently, there were more gender adverts on posters than on bill boards. On each publicity type, the numbers of human images on adverts were higher than non human ones. However, statistical analysis, using chi square ($\chi^2 = 0.272, p = 0.60$) did not show any significant difference, suggesting that the choice of gendered adverts by brewery companies was not related to publicity type (bill board or poster).

Representation of gender in brewery product types

All the adverts found on bill boards were also represented on posters. Half of the 10 bill board gendered adverts observed during the study were on alcoholic drinks while the other half represented soft drinks. However, of the 53 adverts observed on posters, 30 (56.6 %) advertised alcoholic drinks, while 23 (43.4 %) advertised soft drinks. The Chi square statistic was not significant ($\chi^2 = 0.875, p = 0.34$), suggesting that none of the drink type dominated a particular publicity type.

Table 1 shows the number and percentage of gendered adverts for alcoholic and soft drinks for the different brewery companies in Cameroon. Results show that gender adverts for both drink types was dominated by SABC (64.2 %), followed by GCSA (32.1 %). The chi square statistic was highly significant ($\chi^2 = 9.096, p = 0.01$, df = 2), suggesting that there was an imbalance in gender representation on the adverts of brewery products by the different companies in Cameroon.

This finding rejects the first hypothesis (H1) that gender is equally represented in the adverts of brewery companies in Cameroon. Consequently, while a company, such as SABC uses gender to advertise most of its products, UCB did not consider associating gender in the advertisement of its alcoholic drinks (Table 2).

Table 1: Number (and percentage) of gender adverts of three brewery companies in Cameroon

Drink type	SABC	GCSA	UCB	Total
Alcoholic drinks	66.7	33.3	0.0	100
Soft drinks	60.9	30.4	8.7	100
Total	64.2	32.1	3.7	100

Figures in parentheses are percent representations of drink type analysed. $\chi^2 = 9.096$ ($p = 0.01$, df = 2)

The gendered adverts in brewery products were analysed for male and female representations. Each gender advert was considered for presence of male, female or both representations. The study showed that, of the 30 gendered adverts of alcoholic drinks, 14 (46.7 %) represented males alone, 4 (13.3 %) represented females alone while 10 (40 %) represented both sexes. On the other hand, of the 23 soft drink adverts, only 4 (17.4 %) represented males alone while 8 (34.8 %) represented females alone and 11 (47.8 %) represented both sexes (Table 3). These data were supported by a highly significant chi square test ($\chi^2 = 23.7$, $p < 0.001$) which indicates an imbalance in the representations of males and females in the advert of both drink types.

This finding confirms the second hypothesis that male and female models are unequally represented in the adverts of brewery products (alcoholic and soft drinks) in Cameroon. Hence male models were more sought in the advertisement of alcoholic drinks while female models were more encountered in those of soft drinks (Table 2).

Table 2: Number (and percentage) of male and female representations in the adverts of alcoholic and soft drinks in Cameroon

Drink type	Male	Female	Both	Total
Alcoholic drinks	14 (46.7)	4 (13.3)	12 (40.0)	30 (100)
Soft drinks	4 (17.4)	8 (34.8)	11 (47.8)	23 (100)
Total	18 (34.0)	12 (22.6)	23 (43.4)	53 (100)

Discourses found in the adverts of brewery products

There were 25 appearances of male models and 18 of female models in alcoholic drinks adverts, while in soft drinks adverts male and female models appeared 15 and 18 times respectively. Each gender advert was scrutinised for all the outlined themes based on the most probable message or action portrayed. The common themes portrayed in the different adverts were subdivided into (i) agentic, dominant and active portrayals, (ii) secondary role portrayals, (iii) sexual theme portrayals, and (iv) other theme portrayals.

Agency

Table 3 shows the gender portrayals of dominant, active roles in the adverts of both drink types. In the adverts of alcoholic drinks, 25 depicted male roles and 18 female roles while in those of soft drinks, 15 depicted male roles and 18 female roles. The analysis of adverts for foregrounding or main role showed that male models played main roles than female models (84.0 %) in alcoholic drinks (44.4 %) while both sexes were equally represented in soft drink adverts.

The analysis of the adverts for strength, power and agility portrayals showed that male models (52.0 %) dominated these roles in the adverts of alcoholic drinks as compared to female models (5.6 %) while in the adverts of soft drinks, these roles were played by 26.7 % and 33.3 % for male and female models, respectively.

The Chi square statistic was highly significant (χ^2 = 13.51, p <0.003, df = 3), indicating a significant disparity in the portrayals of these functions for male and female models in the adverts of brewery products. This confirms the third hypothesis (H3) that males take more agentic, dominating and active roles than women in the adverts of alcoholic drinks while females played lead roles in soft drink adverts. It also answers research question 3 that male models are foregrounded in the different roles depicted in the representations.

Consequently, in these adverts, men were more associated with strength and power responsibilities which involve some sort of achievement or overcoming challenges. Men were usually portrayed as virile, muscular and powerful, whereas women were presented as playing passive roles (Table 3).

Table 3: Number (and percentage) of dominant and active themes portrayed by male and female models in the adverts of alcoholic and soft drinks in Cameroon

Major theme portrayed	Alcoholic drinks		Soft drinks	
	Male	Female	Male	Female
Foreground, main role	21 (84.0)	8 (44.4)	10 (66.7)	11 (61.1)
Strength, power, agility	13 (52.0)	1 (5.6)	4 (26.7)	6 (33.3)
Total no. of adverts	25 (100)	18 (100)	15 (100)	18 (100)

Figures in parentheses are percent representation of the themes analysed. $\chi^2 = 13.51$ ($p < 0.003$, df = 3)

Gender portrayal of secondary role themes in the adverts of brewery products

Gendered adverts were analysed for portrayals of secondary roles, such as licensed withdrawal, decorative poses, submissive and passive stance, back grounding and dependence (Table 5). Licensed withdrawal by female models (models seemed to be drifting off, gazing away from the camera, engaging the viewer with seductive eye contact or a sexually seductive look) was represented by 55.6 % in alcoholic drink adverts and 44.4 % in those of soft drinks. Male models did not portray any of these themes in the adverts of both drink types.

Female models portrayed in backgrounded roles as entertainers, or models posed as cute and girlish (smiling and/or giggling), or in secondary functions were often represented as being part of a context (family, friends, colleagues) and working/thinking as part of a team (dependent), against men portrayed as more bold and independent. Secondary roles were portrayed in 50.0 % of female models as against 12.0 %of males for alcoholic drinks and 33.3 % for females as against 26.7 % for male in soft drink adverts. The analysis of the adverts for dependent roles was similar to the above observations (Table 4).

The chi square analysis was highly significant ($\chi^2 = 84.34$, $p < 0.0001$, df = 12), suggesting that male and female models portrayed distinctively different roles in the adverts of both drink types. Consequently female models portrayed secondary roles, such as licensed withdrawal, decorative poses, submissive and passive stance, backgrounding, especially in the adverts of alcoholic drinks. This further confirms the third hypothesis that male models are fore grounded in the different roles depicted in the representations.

Table 4: Number (and percentage) of secondary role themes portrayed by male and female models in the adverts of alcoholic and soft drinks in Cameroon

Major theme portrayed	Alcoholic drinks		Soft drinks	
	Male	Female	Male	Female
Licensed withdrawal	0 (0.0)	10 (55.6)	0 (0.0)	8 (44.4)
Decorative poses	3 (12.0)	11 (61.1)	4 (26.7)	16 (88.9)
Submissive and passive stance	0 (0.0)	10 (55.6)	0 (0.0)	10 (55.6)
Background, secondary role	3 (12.0)	9 (50.0)	4 (26.7)	6 (33.3)
Dependent	2 (8.0)	15 (83.3)	2 (13.3)	10 (55.6)
Total no. of adverts	25 (100)	18 (100)	15 (100)	18 (100)

Figures in parentheses are percent representations of the themes analysed $\chi^2 = 84.34$ ($p < 0.0001$, df = 12).

Gender portrayal of sexual themes in the adverts of brewery products

Adverts were coded for gendered representations, such as gaze (object or subject of gaze), nudity and erotic content portrayal (Table 5). In most adverts, female models were more represented as objects of gaze unlike male models. Adverts within this category reflected the concepts of the 'only body trope', namely, that a woman has only her body to offer. In this category, the concept is made more specific as women are told to use their bodies to get what they want. This value was represented in 77.8 % of alcoholic drinks and 72.2 % in soft drink gender portrayals.

Characters were observed as the object of another person's gaze. This happens when somebody poses for camera and (often) assumes a submissive or passive stance usually with lowered eyes and a head down position. This was more common with female images (55.6 % in both drink types) while male models did not portray any of these characters in the adverts (0.0 %).

Characters were also identified for sex appeal poses, whereby the presence of a physically attractive and sexy man and woman was unrelated to the advertised product. The focus was on their body rather than the product; thus as sex object. In this category, female representation was 61.1 % as against 12.0 %for males in alcoholic drinks and 26.7 % for male as against 88.9 % for females.

Sexually provocative and suggestive contents object were defined as being depictions of women as sexual beings whose main function in the adverts was to be erotically enticing. Sexual elements in adverts with visual and overt female nudity and erotic content were observed in 10.7 % of portrayals. In alcoholic drink adverts, 38.9 % adverts contained seductively dressed models for females as against 4.0 % for male while for soft drink adverts 16.7 % of female adverts contained at least a hint of sexual suggestion with emphasis on sexuality and sexual availability as against 0.0% for male for adverts. Chi square was highly significant (χ^2 = 19.97, p = 0.002, df = 6), suggesting that gender representation on sexual themes in the adverts were not randomly chosen. This further confirms the above hypotheses.

Table 5: Number (and percentage) of sexual themes portrayed by male and female models in the adverts of alcoholic and soft drinks in Cameroon

Major theme portrayed	Alcoholic drinks		Soft drinks	
	Male	Female	Male	Female
As a sight to be gazed upon	2 (8.0)	14 (77.8)	4 (26.7)	13 (72.2)
Object of another person gaze	2 (8.0)	13 (72.2)	4 (26.7)	15 (83.3)
Nudity and erotic content portrayal	1 (4.0)	7 (38.9)	0 (0.0)	3 (16.7)
Total no. of adverts	25 (100)	18 (100)	15 (100)	18 (100)

Figures in parentheses are percent representations of the themes analysed. χ^2 = 19.97 (p = 0.002, df = 6)

Gender portrayal of other roles in the adverts of brewery products

The gender adverts were also analysed for portrayals of other themes, such as prizes to win and sports (Table 6). Results also show a disparity in the portrayals for male and female models in the advert of both drink types as both prizes to win and sportive portrayals were dominated by male models for both drink types. Chi square was highly significant ($\chi^2 = 14.22$, $p = 0.003$, df = 3), suggesting that gender representation of these themes in the adverts were not randomly chosen.

Table 6: Number (and percentage) of other roles portrayed by male and female models in the adverts of alcoholic and soft drinks in Cameroon

Major theme portrayed	Alcoholic drinks		Soft drinks	
	Male	Female	Male	Female
Prizes to win	12 (48.0)	6 (33.3)	4 (26.7)	4 (22.2)
Sportive portrayal	8 (32.0)	3 (16.7)	3 (20.0)	0 (0.0)
Total no. of adverts	25 (100)	18 (100)	15 (100)	18 (100)

Figures in parentheses are percent representations of the themes analysed. $\chi^2 = 14.22$ ($p = 0.003$, df = 3)

Discussion

The above portrayals show the discrepancy in the representation of male and female models in the adverts of brewery products in Cameroon. These representations support the fourth hypothesis that gender representation is a reflection of the societal ideologies and stereotypes.

The results of gender representations in adverts indicated that not all companies used human images to advertise their products. Moreover, the finding rejects the first hypothesis that gender is represented equally in the adverts of brewery companies in Cameroon. Enow-Arrey and Ngoasong (2005) also reported an imbalance in the proportion of adverts used in the marketing of brewery products in Cameroon. This is because the female gender is not always considered in public and is thus underrepresented.

Furthermore, it was realised that within gender adverts, there was a highly significant imbalance in the representation of male and female models in the advert of both alcoholic and soft drinks. It was realised that advertisers give preference to male models than females especially in beer adverts. A similar result has been reported by Strate (1992) in USA. In the same line, Limpinnian (2002) found that men not only dominate the workplace but directors in general are men especially the advertising directors in companies. This brings to light the hegemonic ideology that the Cameroonian society holds tight to, that men are more efficient, intelligent and more active. Limpinnian (2002) also observed that we are surrounded by a patriarchal mass media and this is why Kellner (2003) reported that adverts are everywhere and used to each company's advantage so as to maintain the societal stereotypes.

In terms of gender variety in roles representations, it was found that the adverts did not actually represent enough of a range of men and women. Women were not being depicted in wider range of social and occupational roles. Men continue to see themselves as powerful, leaders, managers of people, breadwinners, sexually aggressive, authoritarian and not domestic helpers, caregivers, or partners to their women folks (Lysonki, 1983). The reverse is also true for women, as they are generally depicted as minors, passive, incompetent, dependent and not partners to men. All such stereotypes distort how the different genders see each other and what is accepted as desirable for men or women. In another study, Limpinnian (2002) reported that 67 % of people believe that television advertising's portrayal of men and women is not an accurate reflection of societal values.

The discourses drawn from the adverts show that men were foregrounded and associated with strength, power, independent, active and sportive (as sports, which involve some sort of achievement or overcoming challenges), whereas women are backgrounded and presented not only as dependent, in decorative and submissive posses but also weak and vulnerable. These representations consequently depicted what maleness or femaleness stands for within the Cameroonian society and culture. Zimmerman and Dahlberg (2008) reported that in the USA women still consider that adverts treated them mainly as sex objects, showed them as fundamentally dependent element, and found the portrayal of women in adverts to be offensive. Moreover, these findings are consistent with previous reports that women are often depicted as housewife, decorative element, sex object, concerned with physical attractiveness, and dependent on men (Lysonski, 1983; Ferguson *et al*, 1990; Henthorne & La-Tour, 1995; Mayne, 2000; Zimmerman & Dahlberg, 2008). The image is intended to illustrate an opposition between strength and weakness. This binary gender differences is exactly what some post modernist like Cameron

(2005) are combating in gender portrayals. They consider it old fashion and feel that a paradigm organised around the concept of binary differences has been superseded, for the most part, by one that is concerned with the diversity of gender identities and gendered practices. I procure this idea and assert that women are not only to be constructed as fragile, dependent etc but that some women not only play some of these dominant roles in our society, but also take part in other diversified functions compared to men. Moreover, Strongin (2008) with the same view reported that men and women are presented differently as those who are not the same and are targeted by diverse social norms and stereotypes, some of which are reflected in the power of advertising and in its ability to manipulate people.

Models used in the adverts were Cameroonians or Africans dressed in varied fashionable western attires. This suggests the openness with which Cameroonians embrace globalisation and would like to stay current in fashion. Atanga (2007) cautioned the fact that globalisation apart from having positive contributions to the society, also could be a problem to both men and women. Cameroonians have had the inclination to copy foreign practices as seen in the adverts. This is against the Cameroonian cultural and traditional expectations of women as regards dress code and social practices. This is contrary to the stereotype of a model African woman who is supposed to dress modestly without exposing her body in order not to be termed a prostitute or sexual objects (Atanga 2007). This is not only a Cameroonian ideology as in the USA, Frith *et al* (2004) reported that western women are used as sex objects in advertising across cultures. In some of the pictorial depictions on the adverts of brewery products in Cameroon, part of the female body (legs, breasts, etc) was displayed. This places prominence on her body parts and presupposes and denigrates women as sexual objects whose aim is to satisfy the sexual instincts of men. Women were constructed here as a sight to be gazed upon. Some authors also report that women are portrayed in adverts as the object of another person's gaze, reiterating that their bodies are their best asserts (Soley & Kurzbad, 1986; Lukas, 2007). Zimmerman and Dahlberg (2008) found the portrayal of women in advertising to be offensive since adverts treat them mainly as sex objects and showed them as fundamentally dependent elements. However, several feminist groups criticise representations of women on billboards or posters displayed as sex objects or as passive rather than active agents (Hogan, 1997).

Examining the effects of sexual objectification in adverts on consumers, Zimmerman and Dahlberg (2008: 74) found that it leads to sexual aggressive and experimentation, increased rate of teenage pregnancy and STDs. In another study, Atanga (2007) established that according to the social norms of Cameroon, women are constructed as beings that ought to be relatively 'invisible' in public and not allowed to display evidence of their sexuality, as this may be perceived as 'flaunting' it and that publicly visible women risk being seen as prostitutes, accordingly bringing woes on themselves. Atanga cited *a Swahili/Fulani proverb that says 'For a woman, display is dishonour'*. This controversy was reported by Lanis and Covell (1995), who affirmed that the irony of the latter representation is that the very qualities that women are encouraged to develop (beauty, sexiness, passivity and powerlessness) in order to meet cultural ideals of femininity contribute to their victimization. Moreover, the qualities that men are urged to exemplify (aggressiveness, dominance, sexuality and strength) are identical to those linked to the abuse of women. Lanis and Covell (1995) concluded that by presenting women exclusively as sexual beings, a power differential is created in which women generally are subordinate.

Contrary to traditional discourses, another form of discourse found in the study revolved around the subversive/progressive portrayal of women. An explanation could be found in the feminist theory which is based on Western liberalism and Western concepts of human rights. For example, Frith *et al* (2004) reported that according to this theory, in Western cultures women have acquired certain rights in relation to their bodies in what they wear and even to have pleasure in public places which was traditionally a male domain, where women could only traditionally be brought by their husbands if not they were positioned as prostitutes where prostitution is not only criminal but seen as immoral. This brings about renunciation to traditionally hegemonic and patriarchal constructions of masculinity in Cameroon. Media through these portrayals can have a positive effect on women as Endeley (2004) supports that those who uncritically follow the dictates of media culture tend to 'mainstream' themselves, conforming to the dominant fashion, values and behaviour. The results of this study lend credence to these concerns. Consequently, postmodernists as Cameron (1997) and Butler (1990), advance this idea by purporting that gender can only be defined in its performative function.

In testing the hypothesis that gender representation is a reflection of the societal ideologies and stereotypes, I realised the hypothesis was accepted in the Cameroonian context. Atanga (2007) described Cameroon as a country caught between two civilizations with competing ideologies: traditional vs. contemporary (progressive) and also identified discourses that articulate the construction of model traditional Cameroonian women and men as 'subject' to the roles traditional society ascribes to them (or have 'subject positioned' them). These are binary stereotypes where stereotypical masculinity, for instance, is portrayed as natural, normal and universal, but it is in fact a particular construction. This is similar to the view of Chandler (2007) that advert images largely reflect traditional patriarchal notions of gender.

These results confirmed the stereotypical representation of gender relationships in Cameroon. Some of the stereotypes realised in the adverts are: i) women are the weaker sex, ii) women are dependent on men, iii) men are powerful, etc. Litosseliti (2006) also established that media reflect cultural values and ideals about gender. My findings are in support of this claim as the brewery adverts portray women, men, and relationships between the sexes in ways that mirror widely shared understandings and ideals of the Cameroonian society. I therefore claim that the asymmetric gender representation in the adverts of brewery products in Cameroon is a reflection of the societal ideologies and stereotypes.

Conclusions

A majority (58.9 %) of adverts of brewery products in Cameroon contained human images although the choice of gender adverts by brewery companies was not related to publicity type (bill board or poster). The gender adverts for both alcoholic and soft drinks was significantly dominated by SABC, followed by GCSA and UCB, suggesting an imbalance in the gender adverts of brewery products by these companies in Cameroon. This finding rejects the hypothesis that gender is equally represented in the adverts of brewery companies in

Cameroon. Consequently, while a company, such as SABC uses gender to advertise most of its products, UCB did not consider associating gender in the advertisement of its alcoholic drinks.

A majority (56.6 %) of the gender adverts were on alcoholic drinks, compared to 43.4 % for soft drinks. However, the Chi square statistic was not significant, suggesting that none of the drink type dominated a particular publicity type.

There was a highly significant imbalance in the representations of male and female models in the advert of both drink types. This confirms the hypothesis that male and female models are unequally represented in the adverts of brewery products in Cameroon. Hence males were more sought in the advertisement of alcoholic drinks while females were more encountered in those of soft drinks.

Male models significantly portrayed dominant and active roles depicting strength, power and agility than female models. This confirms the hypothesis that male models take more agentic, dominating, active and sportive roles than female models in the adverts of alcoholic drinks while females play lead roles in soft drink adverts. Contrarily, female models significantly portrayed secondary roles in the advert of both product types such as licensed withdrawal, decorative poses, submissive and passive stance, back grounding and dependence. Consequently, female models were portrayed in background and dependent roles as against men portrayed in more bold and independent. Female models also significantly portrayed sexually connotative roles, such as gaze (object or subject of gaze), nudity and erotic content and sex appeal poses. This suggests that gender representation on sexual themes in the adverts were not randomly chosen as particular roles were assigned to female models. These findings also support the hypothesis that gender representation is a reflection of the societal ideologies and stereotypes.

Quantitatively, the portrayal of both men and women in adverts was largely traditional and stereotypical, thereby promoting a polarization of gender roles. Although men are generally constructed within the Cameroonian society through powerful and dominant gendered discourses, the analyses showed that Cameroonian women are not always powerless as they tend to challenge, contest and resist these relations in some few cases.

References

Atanga, L. L. (2007). *Gendered Discourses in the Cameroonian Parliament.* PhD Thesis. Lancaster: University of Lancaster.

Butler, J. (1990). *Gender Trouble: Feminism and the Subvention of Identity.* London: Routledge.

Cameron, D (1997). Performing gender identity: Young men's talk on the construction of heterosexual masculinity. In S. Johnson and U. Meinhoff, eds. *Language and Masculinity.* Oxford: Blackwell. pp 86-107.

Cameron, D. (2005). Language, gender and sexuality: current issues and new directions. *Applied Linguistics* 24 (4): 482-502.

Chandler, D. (2007). *Semiotics: The Basics.* London: Routledge.

Deachun, A. (2003). Content Analysis of Advertising Visuals in the Magazine Advertisements: The Roaring Twenties and the Great Depression. (Accessed 7 Dec 2011)

Endeley, J. (2004) Gender mainstreaming through the media: Gender Analysis of the Media and Challenges to Mainstreaming. Communication workshop on "Gender Mainstreaming through the media". The Cameroon Association of Commonwealth Journalists. Mutenguene, Fako Division, Cameroon. 22 March 2004,

Enow-Arrey, E. L. and NGOASONG, Elvis Ngulefac (2005). *The Beer Market in Cameroon.* Master Thesis. Mälardalen University, School of Business.

Ferguson, G.H., KresheL, P.J. and Tinkham, S.F. (1990). In the pages of MS: Sex role portrayals of women in advertising. *Journal of Advertising* 19 (1): 40-51.

Frith, K. T. (1998). How to read adverts http://www.ltcconline.net/lukas/gender/background/howto.htm. Accessed 6 Dec.2011)

Frith, K. T., Cheng, H. and Shaw, P. (2004). Race and beauty: A comparison of Asian and Western models in women's magazine advertisements. *Sex Roles* 50 (1/2): 53-61.

Goffman, E. (1976). *Gender Advertisements.* New York: Harper & Row.

Henthorne, T.L. and La-tour, M.S. (1995). A model to explore the ethics of erotic stimuli in print advertising. *Journal of Business Ethics* 14 (7): 561-69.

Hogan, S. (1997). Problems of identity: deconstructing gender in art therapy. *In: Feminist Approaches to Art Therapy.* Susan HOGAN (ed.). London: Routledge. pp 21-48.

Horsely, R (2007): Representation of femininity and masculinity. www.gender-in-advertising.html. (Accessed 26 May 2009).

Kellner, D. (2003). Cultural studies, multiculturalism, and media culture. Gender, race, and class in media. *www.ltcconline.net/lukas/gender/ pages/nympho.htm. (Accessed 27 May 2009).*

Lanis, K. and Covell, K. (1995). Images of women in advertisements: effects on attitudes related to sexual aggression. *Sex roles* 32: 639-649.

Limpinnian, D. (2002). The portrayal of men and women in TV ads. www.aber.ac.uk/media/.../del0001.html. (Accessed 12 April 2012)

Litoseliti, L. (2006). Gender and Language: Theory and Practice. *London: Hodder Arnold.*

Lukas, A. (2007). Body as tool in the gender ads project: Gender.comAds. www.genderads.com. (Accessed 12 April 2012)

Lysonski, S. (1983). Female and male portrayals in magazine advertisements: a re-examination. *Akron Business and Economic Review* 14: 45-50.

Mayne, I. (2000). The inescapable images: gender and advertising. *Equal Opportunities International* 19: 56-62.

MINEFI–DGTPE (2007). Le secteur industriel au Cameroun – 3 1 / 0 3 / 2 0 0 7. www.ubifrance.fr/default.asp?ref=001B0627506A. (Accessed 5 April 2009)

Smith, L. J. (1994). A Content Analysis of Gender Differences in Children's Advertising'. Journal of Broadcasting and Electronic Media, 38(3), 323-37. ttp://www.aber.ac.uk/media/Students/lmg9307.html (Accessed 7 Dec. 2011)

Soley, L. and Kurzbad, G. (1986). Sex in advertising: A comparison of 1964 and 1984 magazine advertisements. *Journal of Advertising* 15: 46–64.

Strate, L. (1992). Beer commercials, a manual on masculinity. *In: Men, Masculinity and the Media. Research on men and masculinities.* Steve CRAIG (ed.), London: Sage.

Strongin, H. (2008). Gender in advertising. *Australian Journal of Arts Administration* vol. 3. no. 4. Spring Advertising Journal. www.gender-in-advertising. html.(Accessed 26 May 2009).

Sunderland, J. (2004). *Gendered Discourses.* New York: Palgrave Macmillan.

Thompson, J. B. (1990). Ideology and Modern Culture. Cambridge and Oxford: Polity Press / Basil Blackwell .

Van Dijk, T. (1998). Ideology: a Multidisciplinary Approach. London: Sage.

Volosinov, V. N. (1973). Marxism and the Philosophy of Language. Translated by Matejka, L. and Titunik, I. R. New York: Seminar Press.

Zimmerman, A. and Dahlberg, J. (2008). The sexual objectification of women in advertising: a contemporary cultural perspective. *Journal of Advertising Research* (Canisius College). pp 71-79.

8

A representation of political agents in Cameroon's newspapers

By Jiogo Ngaufack Caroline Stephanie
University of Dschang Cameroon

Introduction

In the African society, women have mostly been considered as more active in the private sphere (i.e. getting firewood, getting water, cooking, looking after children, domestic responsibilities, etc) and men in the public one (i.e. judicial and political matters, land ownership, etc). But since the late 1990's, women are more and more present in the public sphere. This is partly due to the gender approach which seeks for equal opportunity of representation of men and women in position of decision making. This approach stipulates that it is essential for Africa to take up the challenge of development to include women in decision making; it defends that not doing so, is depriving the continent of 50 % of its human resources (Bunwaree, 2010). Through a discursive representation of gender in some Cameroonian newspapers, Jiogo (2011) came out with the results that men are mostly presented as providers, as those in power whereas women are describe as wives, mothers, sexual objects.

But more and more, women are present in positions of power in media. This is the case of the Cameroonian press. Thus, this article wants to analyse the media representation of these women in power comparatively to that of men in the same position. We seek to know how women as leaders are portrayed in Cameroonian newspapers compared to men and why are they portrayed in such a way. It is about coming out with the different discourses that are presented to refer to men and women in their leadership positions. It is also important to study all the discursive strategies used in these representations and their purpose.

The theoretical framework draws on the Feminist Media Studies. Feminist theories show, according to a synthesis done by Gaye Tuchman (1979), that women are portrayed in a predictable and straightforward manner. Media are commonly perceived as carriers of discourses which tend to reinforce the construction of femininity as being subordinated to masculinity. According to many feminists including Rosalind Gill (2007), the media remains an instrument of patriarchy perceptions but those analyses recognise that they also portray ideas which can contribute to the evolution of mentalities, depending on the context where they are produced.

The media discourses we examine are those of the newspapers. We choose the newspapers because they are a more accessible data for analysis than the other media. There are issues of storage of audiovisual media and sometimes, archives are not even available in Cameroon. The articles studied are taken from *Cameroon tribune*, *Le Messager* and *The Post*. In *Cameroon tribune*, a pro-governmental newspaper, journalists are not always free to state their opinions. Whereas in *Le Messager* and *The Post*, which are private newsapapers, journalists are freer to give their opinions, giving rise to critical discourses favourable to a new civil society. My focus here has been opinions articles, precisely editorials in *Cameroon Tribune* and *Le Messager* and a column named "opinion" in *The Post*. 07 articles out 60 of the June to December 2009 period were talking about politics abroad. The choice of this period is justified by the arrival of women at presidential positions on the continent.

I am going to do a linguistic analysis of the selected articles. The articles are written in English and French; I will do an English translation of those in French. Below is a table presenting the articles used.

Table 1

The Post	Cameroon tribune	Le Messager
Monday June 1, 2009 " the Role Of Women In Dismantling African Totalitarian Regimes", Neba Fuh, N° 1056, p.4 **Friday June 19, 2009** "Presidents, Dictators Attend Late Gabon Leader's Funeral" Associated press N° 1061 p.4 "The Bongo Syndrome", Neba Fuh, N° 1061 p.4	-----------------	**Mercredi 17 juin 2009** « Succession manquée d'un chef traditionnel », Jean Baptiste Sipa, N° 2877 p.2 **Lundi 14 septembre 2009** « Madagascar des mouvances », Alexandre Djimeli, N° 2940 p.2 **Lundi 05 octobre 2009** « Les aventures de Camara », Alexandre Djimeli N° 2956 p.2

The analysis of these data is mainly qualitative based on KrosraviNik's (2010) systematisation of social actors, social action and argumentation analysis in Critical Discourse Studies. KrosraviNik's incorporates some of the widely applied CDA analytical categories used in the Discourse Historical Approach (DHA) (Wodak, 2001, Reseigl and Wodak 2009), and analytical categories proposed by Van Dijk (2009) along with the socio-semantic approach of Van Leeuwen on the representation of social actors (2009). Thus to critically analyse a text, one should examine the textual elements and explain them in a specific context. From this methodological support, the representation of political agents in media discourses will firstly integrate the socio-political context in which they arise, then the different discourses of men and women leaders.

A tumultuous socio-political context

Africa is facing so many crises at the political and social level. There are for example rebellions, manifestations against the powers in place. Fairclough and Wodak (1997, 258) describe discourse as social practice; doing it implies a dialectical relationship between the discursive events and the situations. Thus, to interpret a discourse, one must examine not only the immanent text elements but also explain the context. Discourses are produced in a specific context and they have a meaning if that context is made explicit. Here, I am going to focus on the socio- political context of each of the countries referred to in the newspapers. I will look at Madagascar, Guinea, Gabon and Liberia. In the sections below, I present the different context (backgrounds) of the newspaper articles I will be examining in the paper. The different elements of context presented here have been drawn from the articles and enriched by other.

The Malagasy crisis

The crisis started in December 2008, when the Ravalomanana government closed Viva TV, a station owned by Rajoelina, the Mayor of the capital city, Antananarivo, after it aired an interview with the former President Ratsikara. The government asserted that the speech threatened to "disturb public order and security", while critics viewed the move as a sign of increasing intolerance by the Ravalomanana government of the opposition and opposing media as an effort to curtail the influence Rajoelina. After the closure of the TV station, Rajoelina issued an ultimatum, demanding in the interest of press freedom and democracy that the government allow the opening of Viva TV and others stations by January 13, 2009. In mid-January 2009, Rajoelina initiated what grew into a wave of public anti-government demonstrations in Antananarivo. The anti-government protests swelled in size over subsequent days. Rajoelina labelled Ravalomanana, a dictator and called for further anti-government strike. In late January, the protests turned violent, as elements of the crowd rioted and looted. Reports in the following days suggested that 70 to 80 persons had died during the unrest, most due to crowd stampedes and arson, which the government labelled "civil disturbance which is akin to an attempted coup". On February 3, 2009 Ravalomanana removed Rajoelina from his mayoral office; the sacked mayor continues to demand that the president be ousted. In early March 2009, after the military was used to suppress protests, they were warned that they might take power if the two opposed sides did not resolve their differences. Key military leaders appeared increasingly to lean towards supporting Rajoelina (see Loch and Cook, 2012).

On March 17, 2009, President Ravalomanana announced that he was resigning and transferring authority to Navy Admiral who refused to assume power and the military, subsequently formally recognized the authority of Rajoelina as the president of High Transitional

Authority (HTA). The country's highest court proclaimed Rajoelina's legitimacy the following day and he was inaugurated as presidents of the HTA on March 21. Rajoelina suspended the Parliament which was dominated by Ravalomanana's party. Today Rajoelina is the Head of state of Madagascar. It is to be noted that in 2002, Ravalomanana won elections against Ratsikara; the latter wanted to falsify results; Ravalomanana called the population to rebellion, calling Ratsikara a dictator. Contrary to Ravalomanana, Rajoelina, did not present himself to elections; he uses force to get into the presidential palace, without waiting that the former president mandate expires. ("Madagascar des mouvances" Alexandre Djimeli September 14, 2009 N° 2940). Rajoelina said ravalomanana was not doing well; the latter quits for him to come and do better. But rather than doing better he is dereriorating the situation; he oppresses every public manifestation, refuses any negotiation and takes decisions that means death to his people. As such if there is a dictator here it is Rajoelina.

The Guinean crisis

Captain Moussa Dadis Camara took power in a military coup in December 2008, promising to hold office temporarily while he paved the way for democratic elections and a civilian government (Alexandre Djimeli, les aventures de Camara, october 5, 2009 N° 2956, p. 2. However, Camara swiftly dissolved the government and parliament, suspended the Constitution and forbade union activity. Both the national and international community condemned the coup, and formed the International Contact Group on Guinea, chaired by the African Union and Economic Council of West African States (ECOWAS). The Group also included representatives from CEN-SAD (Community of Sahel-Saharan States), the Organisation of the Islamic Conference, the EU, and the UN to monitor the situation and work multilaterally to restore constitutional order in Guinea. While in power, Captain Camara's party, the National Council for Democracy and Development (CNDD), allowed security forces, under the guise of tax collection and national security, to commit theft and violence against the civilians.

According to the Human Rights Watch, Captain Camara's term in office was characterized by violations of human rights and of the rule of law. Though Captain Camara scheduled democratic elections for 31

January 2010, he went back on his pledge not to run as a candidate to the dismay and dissatisfaction of both the domestic and international communities (ICRtoP). This frustration with the junta and with Captain Camara among the population of Guinea led to public political opposition, culminating in the non-violent protest on 28 September 2009. On 28 September 2009, government forces in Guinea interrupted a peaceful political protest in a stadium in Conakry and opened fire on civilians. The protesters were demonstrating against the alleged plans of Captain Moussa Dadis Camara, leader of the ruling junta, to run in the upcoming presidential elections. According to an investigation by Human Rights Watch, the violence of 28 September 2009 resulted in over 150 civilian deaths, at least 1400 wounded, and reports of widespread sexual violence and rape.

The Gabonese context

Leon M'ba became Gabon's first president with Albert Bernard Bongo Ondimba as vice president in 1960. It is widely known that the French government funnelled a lot of money into his campaign in order to continue their logging exploits in the country. When M'ba took power, it was not long until he abolished all other political parties and took a dictator role. There were widespread riots and an attempt to overthrow the government but the French government intervened and sent the army restore M'ba to power. M'ba remained president until his death in 1967 when vice president Albert Bernard Bongo succeeded him.

Bongo dissolved the current political party and created his own one-party State. In 1973, Bongo was re-elected without opposition and convert to Islam and took the name Omar. He continued until public perception forced him to bring multi-party politics to Gabon in 1990. He was 'elected' as president several times and ruled Gabon from 1967 until he died in 2009. Throughout his rule, there were several claims of fraudulent election results but he remained president for a whopping 42 years (Strobel, 2011). Omar Bongo was widely criticized for doing more for France than Gabon and many people questioned why the wealth from the massive oil revenue was not seen throughout the country when apparently, Bongo had hundreds of millions of dollars in his own bank account ("Presidents, Dictators Attend Late Gabon Leader's Funeral" Associated press N° 1061 p.4). After his death,

Francine Rogombé, President of the Senate was to stand for the Head of State and organise elections for the new president.

The Liberian context

Charles Taylor was elected president of the Liberia in July 1997. In 2001, a report of the United Nations on the traffic of diamonds and weapons in Sierra Leone, where Taylor supports the bloody rebellion, leads to economic sanctions against Liberia; which sanctions were renewed in 2002 and 2003. In February 2002, Taylor decrees a state of emergency when rebels approached Monrovia, after the assault they launched on Guinea and Sierra Leone borders. More and more isolated at international level and militarily weakened, Taylor is charged in June 2003 by a Special Court of United Nations with responsibility in War crimes and crimes against humanity committed in Sierra Leone. Under international and popular pressure, he resigns from power (The Role of Women in Dismantling African Totalitarian Regimes", Neba Fuh, N° 1056, p.4).

In August 2003, during discussion between rebels and the government, they unanimously agreed on the nomination of Gyude Bryant to lead the transitory government. He was to lead the country for two years and organised presidential and parliamentary elections. In 2005, Ellen Johnson defeated a popular soccer player, Georges Weah, to become president. She took over a nation of 3.5 million people that was still struggling to recover from more than a decade of civil war that claimed more than 200,000 lives and displaced a third of the population. When Mr Taylor went into exile in 2003, he left behind a nation shattered by war, with the entire infrastructure, from roads to electric wires to water pipes, rotted away or looted (Moses Gray, 2012). Ellen Johnson Sirleaf is the president of Liberia, the first woman to be elected to lead a country in modern African history. Mrs Johnson Sirleaf was broadly perceived as a reformer and peacemaker when she took office in 2006.

One can see that the socio-political context of each country is peculiar; but they can be grouped in two: popular rebellion for Liberia and Madagascar and death of the former ruler as far as Gabon and Guinea is concerned. Context as a crucial interface between discourse and society plays a fundamental role in Critical Discourse Studies, which are premised on the detail analysis of some of these discourse-society relationships (Van Dijk 2009, p.74). Thus what discourse on men have the journalists presented in our corpus?

Political Representation of Men

Men as African leaders are commonly portrayed in the newspapers as people who do not care for the welfare of those they are ruling and that dictatorship is what characterises them. This main topic is represented in the articles under two sub-topics self-interest fighters and power's eagerness.

Defending Self-interest

Analysis reveals that the representation of self-interest is constructed around four axes: owners of national resources, positive self and negative other construction, investment in foreign countries and the squandering of natural resources.

In, "Succession manquée d'un chef traditionnel" June 17, 2009 in *Le Messager*, Bongo is referred to as "propriétaire du peuple et du patrimoine national" (Excerpt I1a) that is *owner of the people and national riches*. The choice of the word "owner" and the complement added to it "people and national riches" shows to what level he has appropriated them. As the owner, he has no account to give to whosoever. He is free to use his property according to how he wills. The construction of "owner of the people" calls to mind slavery where people were considered as property. Oxford Practice Grammar (1999) stipulates that "and" as coordinator is often used to joined two or more words or clauses of an equal importance. People and national resources in our context refer to belongings that can be used by the owner for their welfare; whatever others may endure.

Through the use of intertextuality, journalists portrayed the selfishness of African in their representation of their self and the other. In "Les aventures de Camara", October 05, 2009 of *Le Messager*, Alexandre Djimeli evokes an interview Dadis Camara has on Rfi (Radio France International) where he presented himself as just having a symbolic and indirect responsibility in the carnage that took place in his country. The people responsible he says are the political men (not women) and the army.

"Dans une interview à Radio France Internationale (Rfi) hier dimanche 04 octobre, le capitaine Dadis Camara admet une responsabilité symbolique et indirecte du fait que, dit-il, il est « le père de la nation guinéenne ». Mais au delà, il estime que seuls les hommes politiques et l'armée emportent la responsabilité directe du carnage de lundi dernier. « Je n'ai pas donné l'ordre de tuer; je n'ai pas évolué dans le sang pour arriver à la présidence », affirme-t-il, comme pour indiquer qu'il est épris de paix. " "Les aventures de Camara", October 05, 2009 of *Le Messager* (Excerpt I1b)

> *In an interview on Radio France Internationale (Rfi) yesterday Sunday 04 October, Captain Dadis Camara admits a symbolic and indirect responsibility because of the fact, he says, that he is the "father of the Guinean nation". But above all, he estimates that only political men and the army are directly responsible for the carnage of last Monday. "I have never given the right to kill. I have not evolved in blood to arrive at the presidency", he affirms as to indicate that he is fond of peace.*

The journalist reports that Camara positions himself as a peace lover and as such he cannot be at the origins of trouble. To convince his hearers that he cannot be the one, he calls on a natural feeling, the jealousy of the other political men who in 50 years were unable to do what he has done in 8 months. He is portrayed as someone who wants development and others as those who are unable to achieve development projects; moreover, they destroyed what he has done.

"Moussa Dadis Camara croit dur comme fer que les hommes politiques qui, en 50 ans d'indépendance ont continuellement enfoncé la Guinée dans la misère, sont jaloux de ce qu'il a pu faire en huit mois. Il pense que c'est eux qui ont lancé les jeunes dans la rue, avec l'intention de déboucher sur un break-up et pourquoi pas, sur un balayage de la junte." "Les aventures de Camara", October 05, 2009 of *Le Messager* (Excerpt I1c)

> *Moussa Dadis Camara, firmly believes that political men who, in 50 years have continuously plunge Guinea into misery are jealous of what he has been able to do in eight months. He thinks that they are the ones who send the youth in the streets, with the intention of leading to a break-up and why not a sweep from the power of the junta.*

Camara does this so that people should stop blaming him and to disgorge their tears of rage on other politicians. This enters his strategy preparing the population to construct a positive image of him as leader, someone able to do in eight months what others could not do in 50 years. Having this conception, they will be ready to accept his candidacy. And as if he feels that the plea to their emotions was not sufficient, he consults the super natural power, God as the only one who can save him from this situation where he is not loved not matter the good he does. He is implicitly presenting himself as Christ in a world that does not acknowledge him as a saviour.

"Au sujet de l'armée qui, pour lui, est coresponsable avec les hommes politiques, le capitaine indique clairement qu'il ne la contrôle pas. « Quand vous héritez d'une armée déstructurée et non hiérarchisée pendant plus d'un demi-siècle, seul Dieu peut vous sauver », jure-t-il. " "Les aventures de Camara", October 05, 2009 of *Le Messager* (Excerpt I1d)

> *Concerning the army which, for him is co responsible with political men, the captain clearly indicates that he does not control it. "When you inherit a non-structured and non-hierarchic army during more than a half century, only God can save you" he swears.*

In this presentation of himself, Camara wants to tell the Guineans that he was sent by God to come and save them from the claws of former political rulers and their dictatorial trend. As such, all those who are still against his candidacy should understand he is "God's choice" and to suffer for them to be saved. In this representation of self and other, one can see that Camara's self-representation is attributed with the good qualities and the others with bad ones. If in portraying the others with qualities, he is so self-centred, one can imagine that it will be worse when it comes to resources. The articles present economic egoism as common in Africa.

African leaders are portrayed as the cause of poverty in the continent. They exploit the natural resources of Africa for their welfare and do not care about the people. In *The Post* "Presidents, Dictators Attend Late Gabon Leader's Funeral", June 19, 2009, it is stated:

"Hundreds of thousands of people lined the streets of Gabon's capital Tuesday to say farewell to late President Omar Bongo, whose flag-draped coffin was paraded through the heart of a nation he was accused of pillaging during four decades of rules." (Excerpt I1e)

Bongo is accused of pillage. This word is used here to show the gravity of what he has done. It also aims at showing the negative consequences of his acts on the country; and what the country has endured for "four decades". In spite of this, the country is still surviving economically and is one of the richest in the sub-region. The reason for this pillage was to satisfy his "foolish" dreams. "Bongo was accused of using his country's riches to fund not only an extravagant lifestyle, but also French campaigns." (Excerpt I1f) The adjective "extravagant" refers to Bongo's lifestyle. One of those 'extravagant' and unnecessary achievements is building a house of about 800 millions in a country where many are unable to have a meal a day. "The state funeral for the 73-year-old Bongo began inside the marble walls of the presidential palace, a towering edifice he spent an estimated 800 millions to build." (Excerpt I1g) The focus is on the characteristic of the presidential palaces: "the marble walls, a towering edifice" lets the reader observe how national resources are used for non-important things.

Squandering his country's natural resources is not only characteristic of Bongo. In "Madagascar des mouvances" September 14, 2009 of Le *Messager*, it can be seen how through a "cellular metaphor" the author described how the population and human assets, are sacrificed.

"La particularité ici, c'est que ces leaders sont, à l'exception d'André Rajoelina, d'anciens chefs d'Etat. Dans les groupes qu'ils dirigent, il y a un noyau idéologique. Mais celui-ci est encerclé comme par une sorte de cytoplasme constitué de gens qui défendent des intérêts particuliers et des positions de rente. Et autour, il y a une membrane cytoplasmique assez résistante ressemblant fort bien à un prolongement armé de la mouvance. Ce sont ces éléments de la membrane qui descendent bruyamment dans la rue, s'affrontent entre eux ou avec l'armée. Ils sont comme des milices. " "Madagascar des mouvances" September 14, 2009 of Le *Messager*, (Excerpt I1h)

> *The particularity here is that these leaders are, except André Rajoelina, former heads of states. In the groups they lead, there is an ideological nucleus. But this one is circled by a sort of cytoplasm constituted of people defending their*

interest and strategic positions. And around, there is the cytoplasmic membrane, resistant enough, resembling an armed extension of the group. These elements of the membrane are those who noisily go down in the streets, confront each other or with the army. They are like militia.

As in a cell, the membrane, the population here, is the main part attacks and which suffers in a fight. Through this "cellular metaphor", one can understand that all the resources are used to save leaders selfishness; even human lives are not spared. It is the elements of the membrane, (the population here) which are sacrificed during the attack. The text refers to them "the militia". The oxford advanced Dictionary sixth edition (2000, p.744) defines militia as "a group of people who are not professional soldiers but who have had military training and can act as an army." They are not professional; thus when they fight against the army (professional), the consequences are catastrophic with many dead as shown in "Les aventures de Camara". However, this catastrophe is nothing to leaders as their interest is preserved; that is why they never hesitate to send them to the streets or to kill them. Neba Fuh in "The Bongo Syndrome", June 19, 2009 of *The Post* deplores the fact that this self- interest is common on the entire continent.

"The Bongo syndrome has eaten up Africa, where small countries like Congo Brazzaville, Equatorial Guinea, Togo, Swaziland and many more, have been on their knees in front of nincompoops in the names of rulers. They squander the resources without pity."(Excerpt I1i)

The phrasal verb "has eaten up" in this excerpt shows how devastating this attitude is to Africa, consuming it as a fire. Moreover, the word "nincompoops" chosen to refer to these leaders, emphasises their stupidity and lack of good judgement.

What is even more painful in this situation is that rather than investing what they had had from the squander of those assets in their countries, these African leaders prefer to go to western countries, leaving their people in abject poverty. Seemingly, they do not want Africans to gain the smallest benefits from those resources; as we know investing in their countries, will help a few citizens to have a job. From "The Bongo Syndrome", June 19, 2009 of *The Post,* one can read "they squander national resources without pity, preferring to inject stolen money into West economies while their countrymen are dying of poverty". (Excerpt I1j) In their preference of western countries to Africa, these leaders desire to make good profit and their individualist conception of life is revealed. Describing one of investment made in France, the Author of "Presidents, Dictators Attend Late Gabon Leader's Funeral", June 19, 2009 in *The Post* refers to it as a "massive real estate holdings, which include at least 37 apartments in Paris alone". The combination of the qualifier "massive" aims at showing how big the building was. Imagining this investment was in his country, it would have solved the infrastructural problems. Through a rhetorical question in this same article, "Is it worth the trouble to amass so much wealth in foreign territories while your people languish in poverty?" these leaders are called to think about this situation and give an answer to themselves. As said above, the journalist is not waiting for an answer; rather he wants these rulers, if they still have a conscience to judge themselves.

In excerpt 1f, it is said that Bongo also used national resources to fund his political welfare, by funding campaigns of past French politicians. In this excerpt of "Succession manqué d'un chef traditionnel" *in Le Messager* of Wednesday, June 17th 2009, it can be understood that he funded these politicians' campaigns to be sure he would be maintained in power.

Il y avait l'ancien espion français. [...] Il était formaté et programmé pour protéger les intérêts de la France tout en brandissant le leurre de l'indépendance. [...] Il y avait un autre Bongo. Celui qui une fois assuré que son pouvoir serait garanti en échange de la protection des intérêts de ses parrains, avait décidé de se constituer monarque. (Excerpt I1k)

> *There was a former French spy. [...] He had been formatted and programmed to protect French interest while brandishing independence illusion. There was another Bongo. The one who, once assured that his power would be guaranteed in exchange of the protection of the interests of its godfathers, had decided to constitute monarch.*

His selfishness has made him to even become an instrument in others' hands to be used as they want. The computer language "format and programme" points out the fact that his personality was deleted and he was now obeying to a set of instruction that make him to perform a particular task, to defend French interest. The love this

African leaders have of material lead them the power eagerness as they want to always use the national wealth for they alone.

Power Mongers

Men's zeal for power is so great that they are ready to use whatever means to accomplish their desire. This can be seen in their ability to seize the smallest opportunity to overthrow the power in place and confiscate it, their determination to use all means to oppress people and their 'eternalisation' in power.

André Rajoelina is presented in "Madagascar des mouvances" September 14, 2009 of Le *Messager,* as an opportunist who takes advantage of a popular crisis to confiscate power. "André Rajoelina affiche aujourd'hui le profil d'un opportuniste qui a pris le raccourci du coup d'Etat populaire pour confisquer les institutions." (Excerpt I2a) *André Rajoelina displays today the profile of an* **opportunist** *who has taken the short cut of a coup d'état to confiscate the institutions.* In using the word "opportunist" which is regularly employed in a disapproving manner to refer to making use of a particular situation to take advantage for him, in a situation that was not planned; the journalist is showing the greed of this ruler. He was not expecting that opportunity, but rather than enjoying it for the time he was to organise elections. Instead of doing that, he was no longer planning to leave power and wanted to benefit from the situation as much as he could for as long as possible. "Sa bande et lui s'accrochent au pouvoir en essayant d'en jouir le plus rapidement possible et aussi longtemps que durera la jungle." "Madagascar des mouvances" September 14, 2009 (Excerpt I2b) *He and his band cling to power while trying to enjoy it as soon as possible and for as long as the jungle will last."* "Band" and "jungle" chose in this sentence refer to the animal world; they have purposely been selected to express the jungle in which the population is, where the most powerful survives.

The first sentence of the article "Les aventures de Camara", October 05, 2009 of *Le Messager,* referring to Dadis Camara helps us to understand that what he is doing is common in Africa; he is just following what his elders and predecessors do: to take power by weapons and confiscate it by ballots. "Il veut tenter le coup d'un Idriss Deby, François Bozizé, Sassou Nguesso: prendre le pouvoir par les armes et le confisquer par les urnes. (excerpt I2c) " *"He wants to try the initiative of Idriss Deby, François Bozizé, Sassou Nguesso :to seize the power by force and to confiscate it by the ballot."*

After the death of General Lansana Conté, he (Dadis Camara) took the power by a hold up with the reason that he was just going to arrange State affairs and quit. "L'homme fort de Conakry a en effet opéré un hold-up sur le pouvoir il y a maintenant 8 mois, après la mort du dictateur Général Lansana Conté." *The strong man of Conakry has in fact operated a hold up on the power 8 months ago, after the death of the dictator General Lansana Conté."*

As time passes, his love of power seems to increase and he was developing strategies to remain in power. "Au fur et à mesure que le temps passé, il se rend compte que le pouvoir est sucré. Depuis environ trois mois il entretient un flou stratégique sur la possibilité d'être candidat à l'élection présidentielle " (Excerpt I2d). *"As time goes on, he realizes that power is sweet. For approximately three months he has maintained a strategic vagueness on his possibility of being candidate to the presidential election.* Through the oxymoron "strategic vagueness", the author is showing the vagueness has an aim. Strategic refers to something done as part of a clear plan that is meant to achieve a particular purpose or to gain an advantage. Vagueness on its part comes from the adjective "vague" which means something not clear in somebody's mind. One understands something cannot be strategic and vague at the same time, unless the vagueness is a strategy. In Camara context, his strategy was to declare his candidacy in a more peaceful context.

The development of strategies of how to remain in power is a common affair in African countries. Firstly, "they [leaders] establish authoritarian regimes and glide them to undeclared monarchies as the years go by, leaving the people to whom power is supposed to belong, helpless, as they survive from the crumbs of the egoistic extravagant rulers." (Excerpt I2e) Going from an authoritative regime to a monarchy is moving from obedience and respect as an expectation to them as an obligation in whatever context. In a monarchy, all those who are against the royal family are either exiled or killed. Under a monarchical regime, the population is called to accept whatever sufferings they endure. (Excerpt I2e), says it, they are called to "survive from the crumbs of the egoistic extravagant rulers". The word "crumbs" here is the expression of how small is the citizen's portion. With such a situation, a temptation to manifest is however hardly suppressed.

And that is what happens in Guinea, some citizens decided to say no to Dadis Camara's candidacy to the presidency as his aim in power was to organise transparent election to which he was not to take part. In fact, after the death of Lansana Conte, former head of State, Camara took power and declared he just wanted to open Guinea to a democratic era. However, looking at the damages caused by his army on those protesting, it is clear that he uses all what is in his power to oppress the population as he no longer dreams of leaving power.

> "Ces jeunes littéralement écrasés par une armée cinglée, déterminée à marcher sur le sang pour faire garder le *statut quo ante*. Le bilan est très lourd. Des sources officielles parlent d'une cinquantaine de morts, tandis que des sources de la société civile guinéenne évoquent plus de cent morts. En tout cas, même si c'était un seul mort, ce serait trop! A coté de ceux qui ont perdu la vie, on parle des femmes violemment violés, des hommes politiques brutalement brutalisés, des manifestants grièvement blessés. " (Excerpt I2f)

> *Those young literally crushed by a crazy army, determined to march on blood to maintain the status quo ante. The outcome is heavy. Official sources talk of about fifty dead, whereas sources of the Guinean civil society evoke more than one hundred dead. In any case, even if it was only one dead it would be more. Besides those who lose their lives, we are talking of women violently raped, political men brutally ill-treated, demonstrators grievously wounded.*

The domination of hyperboles *literally crushed, women violently raped, political men brutally ill-treated, demonstrators grievously wounded* in the depiction makes the situation tragic, and express the seriousness and the gravity of the pains endured by these people. This vivid image presented here, touches the readers' emotions, and portrays how insensitive or inhumane those leaders are when they want to maintain themselves in power by becoming heartless.

All African leaders presented in the newspapers I studied, except Rajoelina, have made more time in power than provided by their

Constitution; this time varies between 20 and 40 years. For most of them, it is either death or Coup d'état that removes them from power. In "Presidents, Dictators Attend Late Gabon Leader's Funeral", June 19, 2009 of *The Post,* the journalist says "Nearly two dozen African heads of State, including several of the continent's strongmen who themselves have ruled for decades, lined up to pay their respects." (Excerpt I2g) The plural form of decades shows that they have ruled for at least two decades, thus at least 20 years. The verb "to rule" employed to describe their action is full of dominance and oppression. Further, in the same article, a clear number of years made by some of these "strongmen" is given; 26 for Paul Biya in Cameroon, 22 for Blaise Compaoré in Burkina Faso; Bongo who died had made 41 years.

This "eternalisation" tendency even goes further; having filled their eagerness for power, they now look at how their children will continue to achieve their egoism even when they die. The greed for power makes these African leaders to totally appropriate it, making it a family asset. For most of them, African politics is increasingly patrimonial and spoils-orientate. In patrimonial systems, power is centralised on one individual applying it for his self-interest and loyal supporters are rewarded and selectively favoured (Van Wyk, 2007). Neba Fuh in "The Bongo Syndrome", June 19, 2009 of *The Post* bitterly regrets that total appropriation: "And before we could realize despots started willing power to their sons, prolonging the sufferings of the African people." Their love of power is so profound that they want themselves, even dead to continue to rule in through their sons.

In the article, "The Bongo Syndrome", concludes with a rhetorical question: "who can conquer death?" to show the powerlessness of human being in front of death no matter how selfish or power hungry they are. The author is implicitly telling them that what they are running after is "an illusion" as they can never really possess it. This rhetorical question is followed by an argumentation that whatever they will do to maintain themselves in power, death will one day defeat them. These representations end with a ray of hope for the population, that even if the population cannot remove them from power, nature will through death. Dictatorial rulers in my corpus are essentially men; having failed to bring Africa under the light of Democracy, there is growing recognition of the untapped capacity of women and women's leadership.

Political representation of women

Women are hardly represented in traditional terms as those who are always in positions of leadership, nor are they always represented negatively; but curiously, discourse on women and politics always shows them as excelling in domains that are new or challenging to them. These terms are always positive. In a context where women are looked upon as a minor sex, just good at domestics' chores and called to be silent in public, women are now, albeit positively as parliamentarians. Political women present in our data are portrayed as hope for Africa's political change and also as example to follow.

Female parliamentarians: hope for Africa

The fifth meeting of the commonwealth ministers in charge of women's affairs (5WAMM) in 1996 endorsed the target of 30 % minimum of women in decision making positions. Coming to reinforce it, the 9th Women's Affairs ministers meeting (9WAMM) in 2010 called on states to honour the target and to maintain it. In the articles analysed, this hope is constructed by journalists around three main ideas.

Firstly, the states are to organise universal and transparent elections. A woman presided over the funeral of the former president of Gabon and hopes are now that the elections she is to organise will be done in a democratic manner. Through the adjectives "universal and transparent", the author is mentions the focus to lay on respect of people's rights to vote (universal) and on honesty (transparent). There was hope that she will not behave as men do. This can be more understood as history tells us that all the elections organised by Bongo since 1990 had always been contested by opposition, claiming they were not transparent. In *Le Messager* of Wednesday June 17th 2009, it can be read "la succession formelle trouvera sa clé dans la campagne et les opérations électorales libres et transparentes." The emphasis laid on the word "transparent" in this text can be seen as a strong desire not to have elections as the previous ones which were not transparent. Ther is also emphasis on the type of elections that are awaited.

However, this hope can only become reality if Francine Rogombé, the President of Senate understands that she is the one to put in place a system where elections will be universal. The Constitution gives the power to the President of Senate, in case the Head of State resigns or dies to organise the elections of the new president. Through the comparison used in the following excerpt, the journalist hopes that this opportunity should be equal to free choice of a leader. "Si Mme Rogombé perçoit la prérogative que lui donne la Constitution gabonaise comme l'opportunité d'ouvrir aux Gabonais les portes d'un choix libre de leurs dirigeants, et s'il ne survient aucune interférence militaire, alors, l'orphelinat du Gabon sera de courte durée." "Succession manqué d'un chef traditionnel" *in Le Messager* of Wednesday, June 17 2009. *If Mrs. Rogombé perceives the prerogative which the Gabonese constitution gives her like the opportunity of opening to the Gabonese the doors of a free choice of their leaders, and if no military interference occurs, then, the orphanage of Gabon will be of short duration.*

The hope expressed above is aimed at preventing the country from entering into a political crisis as it was the case in others countries. When most Presidents died, their countries never find political stability. The last hope that is laid on this female parliamentarian is to avoid an election or a situation that will lead to tragedies that are occurring in neighbouring countries. "On peut penser que la succession politique de Bongo à la tête de l'Etat ne ressemblera pas à celle de Houphouet Boigny, ni à celle de Niassingbé Eyadema, mais s'avérera une véritable alternance du pouvoir républicain." In"Succession manqué d'un chef traditionnel" *in Le Messager* of Wednesday, June 17 2009. *One can think that the political succession of Bongo will neither resemble that of Houphouet Boigny nor that of Gnassingbé Eyadema, but will prove to be a true alternation of republican power.* The implicit truth of this statement is that free and fair elections have not been organised in those countries (Ivory Coast and Togo), that is why they are in crisis. Succeeding in maintaining the political stability of the country, Rogombé will be bringing in a new vision of alternation of republican power. This one will be the "true" one, meaning others have been the fakes as proof, their instability. Looking at Gabon today, one can say Rogombé has largely fulfilled the hope that lies on her. In a situation where Dadis Camera, was unable to lead Guinea to Democratic election, she did well. Women can thus be looked as those who can succeed in leading countries into a republic alternation of power in respect of the Constitution of these countries. And as Heads of State, how are women portrayed?

Women as head of state: an example to follow

In our data, the only African leader, presented positively is a woman: Ellen Johnson Sirleaf, the president of Liberia. Another recent example is the resolve of women of all walks of life under the banner of "the Women Activist in Liberia Mass Action for peace Campaign" who through persistent non-violent demonstration and sometimes unusual strategies like deciding to sex starve their spouses and partners forced the former Liberian dictator, Charles Taylor to come to the peace ... the Accra Peace Talks, in 2003. The result today is the peaceful and democratic Liberia with the first female head of State. *The Post's* "the Role OF [sic] Women In Dismantling Totalitarian Regimes" (Excerpt II2a).

"Democratic" is a polysemic word, but whatever the context, it is connected with equal participation for all. Some definitions of democracy emphasise the processes that underpin democratic governance, such as fair, competitive elections and freedom of speech and information. Others view democracy more broadly in terms of civil and political rights and the distribution of power in society (see the Governance and Social Development Resource Centre (GSDRC) http://www.gsdrc.org./go/topic-guides/political-system/democracy). Significantly, the Universal Declaration states that democracy presupposes a genuine partnership between men and women in conducting the affairs of society" (IPU website, Universal Declaration on Democracy). Describing Liberia as democratic means this country has been able to combine all these conceptions or at least some of the above qualities.

Looking at the structure of the word "peaceful" it is made with the noun 'peace' and the suffix '-ful'. Added to a noun, this suffix means having the quality of that noun; 'peace' is a situation or period of time in which there is no war or violence in a country or an area. Women are promoters of change, but a change in peace, not in violence. (Excerpt II2a) tells us how hard women fought to remove "the former Liberian dictator, Charles Taylor." Rather than using guns, women used non-violent strategies, even though they sometimes use unusual ones like "sex starving their husbands. What they (women) are looking for is that the country should remain peaceful as war only brings destruction; it never builds up a country. Showing the importance of women in a democratic system, the World Bank book (2010, p.12-13) reports that:

Greater women's rights and more equal participation in public life by women and men associated with clean business and government and better governance. Where the influence of women is greater the level of corruption is lower ... women can be an effective force for rule of law and good governance.

Women are presented here as those whose political participation results in tangible gains for democracy, including greater responsiveness to citizen needs, increased cooperation across party, and more sustainable peace. Women are deeply committed to peace-building and post-conflict reconstruction and have a unique and powerful perspective to bring to the negotiating table. Women often suffer disproportionately during armed conflict and often advocate most strongly for stabilization, reconstruction and the prevention of further conflict. Peace agreements, post-conflict reconstruction and governance have a better chance of long-term success when women are involved (Wollack, 2010).

When women are empowered as political leaders, countries often experience higher standards of living with positive developments in education, infrastructure and health, and concrete steps being taken to help make democracy deliver. Using data from 19 member countries of the Organization for Economic Co-operation and Development (OECD), researchers found that an increase in women legislators results in an increase in total educational expenditure Chen (2008).Women are portrayed as those who succeed where their male counterparts has failed.

Conclusion

To conclude this chapter, the representation of political agents in Cameroon varies from one gender to another. One can see that newspapers do not only represent women negatively but that they are also positively portrayed. If men have always been those in power, it is shown that rather than constructing the African continent, they are destroying it. In each context because of selfishness and power mongery, men have failed where women have used equal opportunity and unity to avoid plunging their countries into disaster. Through a study of the use of language, deployed in the articles studied, I have come out with the discourses of men as dictators and women as a hope for good governance. Women, in certain power positions, succeed in managing social change relating to democratic governance better than men in the same positions. The study of these articles leads me to follow Kofi Annan who declared, in 2005 to the Commission on the status of Women that "study after study has shown us that there is no tool for development more effective than the empowerment of women".

This is also a call to more consideration of women as far as power is concerned. Opportunities were given to some few of them and the way they handle them is hopeful for Africa, as they are able to bring smiles where cries were set. I can say that slowly but surely, the African traditional discourse of men only as leaders is being reversed. This process, I think cannot be faster, as it could face a total resistance of men. Nevertheless there is a hope that women will have a word to say in all the political spheres in Africa; taking into consideration their representation in the newspapers, I think their presence could save Africa from a total loss of democracy. Lastly one can note that newspapers do not present how those women in power tackle problems related to gender: journalists have decided not to say a word about it the reason can be that these female politicians do not lay a particular emphasis on it. Women portrayed in my corpus have succeeded where men could not; but one can ask the question whether women will not reproduce men's behaviour if they are more present on the political scene. In other words, can't their attitude be justified by the fact that they want to prove that they are "capable" where men do not more have something to prove?

Cameroon tribune does not talk about these leaders in the period study. It seems not to see it these men as dictators or chooses to ignore it because as a pro-governmental newspaper, it defends the interest of the State. The Cameroonian government cannot depict what is happening as something bad as it is what is done in this country. The Cameroonian head of state is referred to in one of the articles as "strongman", having done about 30 years in power. Cameroonian media displays a progressive discourse towards women. Moreover, they show they are not only interested by national events; they are also sensitive to what happens out of their country. This shows that foreign affairs influence the national opinion. Subsequently, gender questions should be looked at depending on the local specificities, and on a global scale.

References

Bunwaree, S (2010). *Governance, gender and politics in Mauritius.* Mauritius, ELP Publications.

Chen, Li-Ju (2008) "Female Policymaker and Educational Expenditure: Cross- Country Evidence." Research Papers in Economics 2008: 1 Stockholm University, department of Economics, revised, Feb 27, 2008. [http://ideas.repec.org/p/hhs/sunrpe/2008_0001.html].

Fairclough, Norman and Wodak, Ruth (1997). "Critical Discourse Analysis" in Teun Van Dijk(ed) *Discourse as social Interaction (Discourse Studies: A multidisciplinary Introduction* vol 2) London SAGE 258 – 284.

Gill, Rosalind (2007). *Gender and the Media.* Cambridge, Polity Press.

Golder, Matt and Wantchekan, Leonard (2004). "Africa dictatorial and Democratic Electoral System since 1946" *Handbook of Electoral System Design.* Colomer Josep (ed) London: Palgrave.

Gray, Josephus M. (2012). *Five Years of President Ellen Johnson Sirleaf's Administration.* http://www.gnnliberia.com/index.php?option=com_content&view=article&id=2536:liberia-5-years-of-president-ellen-johnson-sirleafs-administration-a-critical-analysis&catid=34:politics&Itemid=54 (consulted on February 19, 2013)

GSDRC website http://www.gsdrc.org./go/topic-guides/political-system/democracy.

ICRtoP. Crisis in Guinea athttp://www.responsibilitytoprotect.org/index.php/crises/crisis-in-guinea, consulted on (February 15, 2013) In *Occasional Paper Series*: Volume 2, Number 1, 20

IPU website /:http:// www.ipu.org./english/home.htm.

Jiogo, Caroline (2011). *Discursive representation in some Cameroonian Newspapers of 2009.* Master Thesis, University of Dschang, Cameroon.

Kevane, Michael (2004). *Women and Development in Africa: How gender works*. LYNNE Riennen.

KhosraviNik, Majid (2010). "Actors descriptions, action attributions, and argumentation: towards a systematization of CDA analytical categories in the representation of social groups" in *Critical Discourse Studies*. vol.7 No1, February 2010, 55-72, Routledge

Ndoumi, Oscar *(1999). Gestion du biculturalisme dans Cameroon Tribune: Etude comparative 1er juillet 1997- 30 juin1998* Yaoundé, ESSTIC.

Poch Lauren and Cook Nicolas (2012). "Madagascar Political Crisis", in Congressional Research Service Report, at www.+crs.+gov, consulted on October 14, 2012.

Strobel, Verena (2011). *Country report Gabon* at   w.w.w bayermlb.de (consulted on February 19, 2013)

Tuchman, Gaye (1979). Women 's depiction by the Mass Media" *Signs*. vol .4, N°3 Spring, pp528-542 published by the University of Chicago Press at http://www.jstor.org/3173399 consulted on January 29 2013

Van Wyk Jo-Ansie (2007) "Political Leaders in Africa: Presidents, Patrons or Profiteers?"

Wodak, Ruth and Meyer, Michael (2009). "Critical Discourse Analysis: History, Agenda, Theory and Methdology" in Wodak and Meyer (ed)   *Methods of Critical Discourse Analysis*, London, Sage.

Wollack, Kenneth (2010). "Women as Agents of Change: Advancing the Role of Women in Politics and Civil Society" Statement before the House Committee on Foreign Affairs Subcommittee on International Organizations, Human Rights and Oversight.

The Post

Monday, June 1,2009 " the Role Of Women In Dismantling African Totalitarian Regimes", Neba Fuh, N° 1056, p.4

Friday June19, 2009
- "Presidents, Dictators Attend Late Gabon Leader's Funeral" Associated press N° 1061 p.4
- "The Bongo Syndrome", Neba Fuh, N° 1061 p.4

Le Messager

Mercredi 17 juin 2009 « Succession manquée d'un chef traditionnel », Jean Baptiste Sipa, N° 2877 p.2

Lundi 14 septembre 2009 « Madagascar des mouvances », Alexandre Djimeli, N° 2940 p.2

Lundi 05 octobre 2009 « Les aventures de Camara », Alexandre Djimeli N° 2956 p.2

9

Taŋkáp System and Matrimonial Issues in Yemba Language

Raul Kassea, PhD
University of Yaoundé I

Introduction

African matrimonial arrangements have been analysed with European economic grids that are perceived as inadequate. The introduction of foreign currencies by colonial powers (German mark, British pound, French franc in Cameroon) in agrarian societies led to the reification of women as "market values" (Comaroff, 1980). Terms such as *bridewealth* and *dowry* only take into account the source and the destination of the transfers, leaving aside as negligible, the dimensions of the content, the context, and the meaning (Comaroff, 1980, 10). Our exploration of the *taŋkáp* marriage system in the yemba language group aims to re-examine certain linguistic terminology and practices that were read by European ethnologists as the commodification of women.

Evans Pritchard (year) noted that matrimonial transfers everywhere have an economical value. They are found in societies where the ratio cost/benefit of the marriage is not balanced for the main stakeholders. The type of payment is determined by the concerned-bride, groom, their families- who is most disadvantaged (Comaroff, 1980, 4). Goody (1973, 17) contests economicist interpretations: "it is the nature of secular social structures and not the commercial logic of matrimonial arrangements that give shape and meaning to these payments". Comaroff (1980, 10) agrees that the fact the exchanges have economic implications does not necessarily mean that they bear commercial or economic inspiration. Beyond obvious loopholes of the "judicial approach", marriage is perceived as a "package of rights" of which matrimonial services are the instruments of production and/or exchange, summarised in the following rights (Comaroff 1980, 18):

- matrimonial arrangements are essential in the legitimating of the union;
- the transfer of the bridewealth marks the alienation of various rights of a woman to her husband and his relatives;
- in patrilineal systems, they determine kinship, wherefrom the bridewealth is the price of the child.
- the payment marks a transformation of personal and social status for the couple, but also for the givers and takers of women, who become relatives.

As claimed, married women have often been seen as property rather than autonomous beings (Hirschon, 1984). We need to question these statements, to reanalyse familiar matrimonial arrangements with specific reference to their semantic and symbolic qualities.

My contribution examines the ethnographic terminology of some aspects of the *taŋkáp* matrimonial arrangements in the *yemba* language, located in the Menoua division, West Region of Cameroon.

For this paper, I ask the following questions: What is the origin, the meaning and the relevance of the *taŋkáp* marriage system as interpreted by colonial literature? How has the meaning of words relating to language changed over time to reflect the commodification of women within the Yemba language group?

The documentary data was gathered as part of empirical material for my doctoral thesis (Kassea, 1987). The topic of women's autonomy called into question the commodification of women as goods traded between men, especially in an era when western currencies did not exist in the local communities. As a native of Fongo-Tongo, a village in the yemba language group, I have had many discussions with my community elders, and with other yemba speakers and researchers. The indigenous concept of *"lewú"* referred to social prestige and honour and was based on the numerous members of the family and material property such as land and cattle. Barter and gifts of local products were the main modes of circulation of commodities. The introduction of foreign currencies, coins and bank notes locally called *"ŋkàp"* brought wealth and terms such as *"ŋgaŋ ŋkàp"* meaning a 'rich person'. The clear distinction between harvesting, picking (e.g. coffee) from plants, and generating money from whatever activity, constitutes a sound case for challenging the accuracy of the yemba *taŋkáp (literally father of money*) matrimonial system (mis)interpreted as the trade of women between men.

Language and meaning in Yemba matrimonial arrangements

In the yemba communities, *to ask for* or *to propose to* a woman for marriage is called *ŋdó meŋgwí*. *To give a woman* as bride is called *ŋgyá meŋgwí*. After a number of services expected from the bridegroom, the marriage agreement is expressed by the girl's family as *ntswé meŋgwí*. The first meaning of the word *ntswé* is to pound, to mash tubers such as cocoyams into a paste, a local delicacy called *apah lah,* or *achu* elsewhere, traditionally served in festive ceremonies. Some yemba speakers have come to wrongly assimilate women to goods, food that is symbolically pounded and exchanged between families.

Looking at local agricultural practices, we discover that to plant seeds spaced out is called *nó máteh* literally plant-throw, while to plant them tightly close is called *nó ntswé*. This second meaning of *ntswé* becomes more logical as bringing close, tightening links between two people, the young couple, and their two families. Marriage creates allies, kinship, brings people closer and unites them, just as pounding transforms different aggregates into a delicious meal.

Another aspect of the yemba cultural area is the *ŋkáp* marriage system. The general meaning of the marriage system is that a woman is married off to a man who does not deliver the indigenous services expected from a groom. Hurault (1962, 39) summarises the principle as follows: "I give you without bridewealth, just pending a simple present, my daughter or a far relative on whom I have *ŋkáp* rights; the boys born from this union are yours, but the girls are mine; when they reach wedding age, it is I who will arrange their marriages, I will receive their bridewealth, I will exchange them or I will marry them too, under the *taŋkáp* regime for my profit and that of my heirs". Women are here shown as the cement of alliances between men. Though so precious to the giver and the receiver of a woman, the *ŋkáp system* gave an opportunity for men of low resources to get a wife and found a family. The moral debt contracted would be compensated over generations. Authors agree on the origin of the *ŋkáp* system. The foh or village chiefs, owners of war captives and slaves, married them off without bridewealth, to warriors, royal descendants, and even ordinary villagers, keeping the right to marry all the female descent of that first union (Tardits, 1960; Brain, 1972; Albert, 1943). The system was later extended to princesses and daughters of polygamous men. The authors list some advantages of the *ŋkáp* system

- a poor man could get married without delivering normally expected services;
- multiple networks of allies were created, bringing closer individuals, families who lived on the same land but came from various regions;
- a slave woman, married to a prince, got social integration and her descent benefited from their father's status;
- "the absolute opposition of a mother (married under the *ŋkáp* system) is supreme" about her daughter's marriage (Hurault, 1962, 44; Tardits, 1960, 20).

Hurault does not acknowledge the *taŋkáp* as the grandfather of the woman married under that system, but Tardits (ibid, 20) clearly explains the relation: "The girls born from a marriage set under the *ŋkáp* system therefore belong to their mother's grandfather, or through a set of transfers of rights in time, to the first person who gave as *ŋkáp* one maternal ascendant of the girl".

Just who is exactly the *taŋkáp*? According to Hurault (ibid, 40) "nkap simply means money. He who has *ŋkáp* rights over a girl is called her *ta ŋkáp* -father for money- the girl is called his *wa nkap*". Hurault does not translate the last words, but Brain (1972, 173; 180) tells us: "The word for the descendants is *azem nkap* –thing of money, money thing-. Albert (1943, 156) writes: "The *ta-cap*, the money father".

How old is the *ŋkáp* system? The cornerstone of the *taŋkáp* vitality is the local religious belief system based on the ancestors' skull cult. Our ascendants are supposed to intercede between the gods and the living beings. Our destinies, blessings or curses lay in the hands of all the departed of our family trees which fully integrate both male and female lineages. Brain (1972, 121) traced "chiefs' rights over ten generations of descendants of slave women"; counting about 30 years per generation, the system could date back to 1672, or earliest to 1822, if we take into account early marriages around age fifteen. Foreign currencies were unknown in the grassfields; barter was the transaction, as testified in 1890 in Douala by exchanges with pearls, cloth, copper bars and guns (von Morgen 1972, 15; Terray, 1982, 140).

Misinterpretations

The translation of *taŋkáp* as "money father / father for money" may seem absurd to us today. Economicist views monetised a trade system still based on free barter where there were no currencies, no standards set for the exchanges people undertook. Foodstuff and other items exchanged kept a symbolic dimension but were not standard values. Tardits (1970, 390) presents the nkap system as "combining the security of the short term investment with the profitability-extension of alliances and consolidation of loyalties- of the long term investment". The institution becomes a process of capitalisation of matrimonial rights over persons. Albert (ibid, 162) sums up: "Thus is the situation: selling, buying, exchanging, inheriting just as for any domestic commodity, slavery".

This reification and commercialisation of women in the *ŋkáp* system is difficult to understand, since the authors cited earlier (Tardits, 1960; Brain, 1972; Albert, 1943) acknowledge that these unions were free of charge, and the giver of women simply retained the right to marry the female descendants for increasing his social networks. Back to the agrarian context of the Bamileke people, let us find out how the misinterpretation came about. Is there another meaning to the word *ŋkáp*?

In the *yemba* language group, there are high and low tones on the same word; so *ŋkáp* basically means to pick, to pluck-fruits for example-, while *ŋkàp* refers to money. Wealth consisting of goods and human resources is said *lewouh,* not to be confused with cash money that came with the colonial era. Books about the Bamileke languages confirm the tones and distinct meanings; Nissim (1977, 91) writes *kap (nkap)*-high tone- meaning to pluck, while *nkapo, nkab*-low tone- means money. Albert (ibid, 147) mentions the expression "*nkap-fouo-mou*- the person who picks the child's medicine".

Speakers and linguists attest the existence of two close words, discriminated by the tone, and meaning to pick and money. One understands that the foreign observer, caring little about the daily obligations of the indigenous people, remembers mostly words that meet his expectations, which are meaningful in his cultural background, thereby confronting 'nkap' - *to pug* in "*nkap-fouo-mou-* with money. In England, during marriage, a woman's legal existence was suspended; she was the husband's property and could hardly own property (Mendelson and Crawford, 1998); the Napoleon code in France upheld men as supreme masters in the private sphere. Could it be otherwise in Africa, in Cameroon?

Learning local languages through the translation of words taken out of their contexts, projecting their social and economic concepts and practices over the exotic tropical cultures, missionaries, and colonisers inevitably transformed local words and practices. Unfortunately, these (mis)interpretations have been reproduced and transmitted to generations of Cameroonians and Africans whose acculturation does not enable them to criticise wrong concepts. Ntagne and Sop (1975, 53; 66) write: *nkap* (high tone) to pick; later we read "*tankapa*: in the slavery era, he who bought a female slave had rights over all her female descent, it is through him that one passed to buy a girl, a fiancée". This reminds us of Albert (1943) who assimilated the *tangkap* to a slave trader who sold women as sheep, "a human herd". The misinterpretations are spelled out in the contradictory writings of the authors cited above. On the one hand they list "*nkap* (high tone) to pick"; in another context, in the earlier slavery centuries, they dump together the term "ta" for father and "nkap" for to pick, and they generate "tankapa" as a buyer and seller of women. Marriages and slavery precede the introduction of western money, so did planting and harvesting as vital activities.

Further reflecting about the quasi-homonymy of to pick and money in the yemba language, we see the Bamileke farmer as harvesting the fruit of his hard work. Blue or white collar wage labour was the privilege of few people. The foreign currencies were probably assimilated to what a peasant could pick from soil or from his trees, especially the cash crop plants. Selling these local products was the main source of foreign and rare money; barter was less practiced as everybody wanted to buy imported commodities. The expression *ŋkáp ŋkàp* meaning to pick coffee berries illustrates the metonymy: coffee was the most popular cash crop, and thus became the symbol of money, the money tree. Even in the 60s, I could hear my father's wives say: *"Mpeh weuh nka ŋkáp ŋkàp"* meaning "let's go to the (coffee) farm to pick money".

Reinterpretations

The colonial ethnographic work was conducted in a transition era. In the matrimonial commitments, the symbolic local products and services were meant for the fiancé to show that he was brave, hard working, and capable of fending for his family, in collaboration with his wife. A woman was literally begged for, given and united to another family. Reconsidering the word *ŋkáp* as to pick, the *taŋkáp* is a man who builds a secondary lineage by freely giving a female slave or a daughter for marriage. The descent constitutes a family tree from which he literally *picks* girls and marries them to whom he chooses, with the objective of extending his alliances, his descent, the only real pre-colonial wealth. We therefore see the *taŋkáp* as the "father picker, the father maker of allies, the father wedder" of the girls descending from the first woman married off for free by some ancestor, without requiring the traditional services.

Brain (1972, 11) somehow supports our hypothesis or interpretation, as he writes about "marriage lords"; but he is mostly preoccupied by "monetary interests" of the wedders he calls "Lord Money or Lord Bridewealth"; he however acknowledges the symbolic character of the services: palm oil means friendship, salt is gentleness, helpfulness (ibid, 115); there are also hoes for women's tilling; those items were the essential requirements prior to the introduction of the foreign currencies. If a mother did not accept the betrothal log brought by a suitor, if she refused the salt or palm oil, then there could be no wedding. A mother was therefore part of the matrimonial decision-making, not just a commodity in men's hands. Pradelles de Latour (1986, 258; 555) confirms the "symbolic debt" of the Bamileke matrimonial alliance because "the given object is vested with a unique and asymmetric value which, introducing a debt, subdues the receiver to the giver"; the value of a woman is immeasurable. In Bangoua, 57% of women were married in the "bridewealth" system, while 43% had been "given" by a *ta nkap* (ibid, 507).

Concluding remarks

The ever extending networks of *taŋkáp* lineages has led to their segmentation into new autonomous branches. On 4th April 2009, we attended in Fongo-Tongo, the funeral of a man deceased at 82 years old. His last endeavour was negotiating his *taŋkáp* rights, so that his descent would not be burdened by the *taŋkáp* on whom he had depended all his life. It costs symbolic offerings such as stools, garments, food, drinks, and some cash money to obtain the transfer of the *taŋkáp* rights over your own descent and/or a segment of the lineage. In a similar vein, this author personally underwent a ceremony for the transfer of *taŋkáp* rights, on 9th July 2009, so my descent is freed from the indigenous obligations towards the current heir of our acknowledged *taŋkáp*. The historic family links remain, but are somehow weakened. The social rights and obligations of those lineage founding fathers need to be redeemed for a positive understanding of our family trees, the knowledge of where and whom we come from. Unfriendly attitudes and xenophobia would lessen when we discover that someone from a distant village or region is a blood cousin. The current teaching of yemba courses opens opportunities for rediscovering our mother language, its historical and cultural contexts in order to re-appropriate our values, those of our ancestors. The indigenous management of our villages was based on a dual system that fully integrated women; this is still alive as our chiefs appoint both male and female heirs, confirming that women were never commodities for men. The *taŋkáp* system has evolved to retrieve benefits from both male and female descendants; when a man chooses a daughter as main heir, she is automatically entitled to *taŋkáp* rights if her father enjoyed them. Required ritual gifts are thus offered to the heiress who now manages matrimonial arrangements of her *ŋkáp* descent; this reversal of gender roles further attests that the main objective of the *taŋkáp* was not money, but rather the extension of social networks.

References

Albert, R.P. (1943). *Au Cameroun français: Bandjoun*. Montréal: Editions de l'arbre.

Bird, S. and M. Tadadjeu (1997). Petit dictionnaire Yémba- Français. Yaoundé: CELY.

Brain, R. (1972). *Bangwa kinship and marriage*. Cambridge: Cambridge University Press.

Comaroff, J. L. (1980). *The meaning of marriage payments*. London: Academic Press.

Dutcher, N. (2004). *Expanding Educational Opportunity in Linguistically Diverse Societies*. 2nd. ed. Washington, DC: Center for Applied Linguistics. http://www.cal.org/resources/pubs/expand.html

Ethnologue (2009). http://www.ethnologue.com/show_country.asp?name=CM)

Hirschon, R. (1984). *Women and property, women as property*. London: Croom Helm.

Hurault, J. (1962). *La structure sociale des Bamiléké*. Paris: Mouton.

Kassea, B. R. (1987). *Autonomie féminine selon les milieux naturels et culturels*. Unpublished thesis (3è cycle), Université Paris VII, Paris.

Mendelson, S. and P. Crawford, (1998). *Women in Early Modern England 1550-1720*. Oxford.

Morgen von, K. (1972). *A travers le Cameroun, du Sud au Nord, 1893*. Trad. Philippe Laburthe-Tolra. Yaoundé: (n.c).

Nissim, G. (1977). *Je parle Bamiléké*. Douala

Nissim, G. (1981). *Le Bamiléké Ghomala*. Paris: Selaf.

Ntagne, S. & G. Sop (1975). *Manuel de Bamiléké*. Douala: Collège Libermann.

Pradelles de Latour, C.H. (1986). *Le champ du langage dans une chefferie Bamiléké*. Thèse d'Etat, Paris.

Tardits, C. (1960). *Les Bamiléké de l'ouest Cameroun*. Paris: Berger-Levrault.

Tardits, C. (1970). Femmes à crédit. In Pouillon & Maranda (dir), *Echanges et communications*. Paris: Mouton.

Terray, E. (1982). Réflexion sur la formation du prix des esclaves. *Journal des Africanistes*, 1982, 52 (1-2), pp. 119-144.

Section D:
Gender in other contexts

10

How Is the Acceptability Of? An Advertisement Determined?

Anna-Maija Pirttilä-Backman & B. Raul Kassea[10].

In Finland, following ethical regulations on advertisements is largely in the hands of the advertising industry's self-regulation. Regulations concerning advertising are not included in the law on equality, for example. A council for enforcing equality in advertising, The Council of Ethics in Advertising, was founded in 1989. The main duty of the council is to give statements on marketing procedures on request. The statements are based on the regulations of The International Chamber of Commerce. In Finland, the Market Court is the authority that gives verdicts on particular advertisements. In this article we examine the functionality of the current practice by studying the advertisement for *Café Arome* coffee manufactured by Meira Oy and the discussion it evoked. Our goal is to point out the diversity and the ambiguity of the images the advertisement aroused by examining the discussion inspired by it and a small amount of empirical data. We hope this article will inspire further discussion on things such as who should be heard when advertisements are evaluated and how, for example, is offence to human dignity meant to be understood.

During the last years of the 1990s there were many different kinds of coffee advertisements in Finland. One of these was the advertisement for *Café Arome*. It depicts a dark-skinned woman down on her knees with her head resting on her knees. According to a statement given by the Council of Ethics in Advertising (1999) the advertisement for *Café Arome* "uses a naked, brown-skinned female body softened in such a way that the silhouette of the body [forms] an image similar to a coffee bean". The version seen on television was described in the weekly supplement *NYT* (37/1999, 41) of the leading Finnish newspaper *Helsingin Sanomat* as follows: "A coffee bean is transformed into a black dancer and eventually into the steaming aroma of coffee."

---

[10] English translation by Evelina Schmuckli; revised by Raul Kassea.

The advertising industry in Finland follows the regulations of The International Chamber of Commerce. The first version of the regulations was published as early as 1937. These international basic regulations for advertising (1997) aim at promoting a high degree of ethics in marketing through voluntary self-regulation, within the limits of existing legislation. The basic regulations are meant to function as a norm for the voluntary self-regulation of industry and commerce, but they are also available for the courts to be used in interpreting the law. They are applied to the comprehensive content of a particular advertisement including all words and numbers (both verbal and written), images, music and sound effects.

Article 4 of the regulations states: "Advertisements should not condone any form of discrimination, including that based upon race, national origin, religion, sex or age, nor should they in any way undermine human dignity." According to Schein (1996, 18), in jurisprudence discrimination means "unacceptable segregation of people based on their differences" and other activity "which serves to place people in unequal positions". The regulations also state that it is not allowed to play on fear in advertising without justifiable reason.

Evaluation of the advertisement in different contexts

The judicial context

The advertisement for *Café Arome* described above has inspired discussion in many arenas. There is a statement given by The Council of Ethics in Advertising in 1999 available, which was requested by a private person. The Council states that it bases its operation on the international basic regulations cited above. Their opinion is that the advertisement in question "doesn't use the female body in a humiliating or degrading manner. Nudity in itself is not degrading. Therefore, in accordance with the international basic regulations of advertising or the regulations of the Council, the advertisement is not considered to offend equality."

It is interesting to compare this statement with the preliminary ruling made by the Market Court on request of the Consumer Ombudsman in 1994 concerning discriminatory advertising. The court ruled that the consumer protection policy can be applied to discriminatory advertising even though the law does not specifically include regulations on the subject. The law says anything unethical or any methods otherwise inappropriate in regard to the consumer are not allowed in advertising. The court forbade an advertisement that clearly used an image of a woman to catch people's attention without a woman having any connection to the product being marketed as unethical. It was decided that the advertisement is offensive to gender and degrading.

The context of a public/advertising community

The advertisement for *Café Arome* was nominated for the best Finnish television commercial in 1998. A jury of professionals in advertising and in the audio-visual industry chose 30 commercials for the competition and *NYT*, the weekly supplement of *Helsingin Sanomat* (issue 3/1999), published the comments of three people on the coffee advertisement in question. Visa Heinonen, who is working on a book about the history of advertising in Finland[11], said he thought the commercial was stylish. Advertising designer Hannu Konttinen said: "Done in good taste, damned beautiful, emphasizes human beauty. The African drums are amazing, the whole planet uses them. This gave me a good feeling. Many good ideas go wrong when the right degree of activeness isn't found." Consumer Ombudsman Erik Mickwitz was of the opinion that "the commercial is not discriminating in any way, not in regard to women or race. It is done with respect. A black model was used discreetly."

Formulating the study question and justifying it

Formulating the question for this article had its origin in the fact that despite the public discussion with its assurances of beauty and correctness described above, the *Café Arome* advertisement was considered oppressive and offensive as well as beautiful in everyday casual conversation. A Finnish woman who had experienced physical violence felt the advertisement was oppressive: a woman humble on the ground, awaiting the next blow. An African man who had worked alongside his mother in the coffee fields as a child felt that a woman of his continent, which had suffered from colonialism in the past, was still

---

[11] Translator's note: The book was published in 2001 after the original article was written.

being exploited as she was offered as an object to "be enjoyed in a Western coffee parlour". Overall the advertisement inspired conflicting emotions. It was seen as beautiful and as offensive at the same time, but people were often unable to analyze the latter feeling in detail. This is why we began to examine the mental images the advertisement inspires in a group of people somewhat larger than our friends and acquaintances. In other words we wanted to expand the discussion on the advertisement beyond the sphere of professionals in advertising and equality jurisprudence to include the interpretations of people outside it.

The method

The students attending a course included in the subject studies of social psychology at the University of Helsinki were chosen as respondents. There were 42 students, six of whom were male. Their age varied from 18 years to 45 years and their average age was 26.

The study

A slide of the image in the advertisement on loan from Meira Oy was projected on a screen in a lecture hall. The picture on the slide was the same that had been seen in magazines and on posters. We are unable to make the lecture hall completely dark when we showed the image to the students, so it was dimmer than on paper. The students were given empty answer sheets to write down what they saw in the picture and what images it inspired in them. No other instructions, information on the picture or on the goal of the study was given at this stage. The respondents were told that they might have seen the picture before. Our aim was to collect associations and images from the respondents that were as spontaneous as possible.

After the first stage of the study the respondents were given additional information. They were told that this was an advertisement featuring the image of a woman and that some people had seen the picture as racist and sexist. In other words we activated a certain frame of reference in the respondents' minds. Our aim was to find out how easily their ideas would change to fit the frame of reference given. We tested whether they would see more offensive content in the picture after being given this information than before it. However, we did not ask them to try and interpret the picture as racist or sexist. After receiving the additional information, the respondents were asked to write down any new ideas, associations and comments they might have. They were also asked to write down their age and gender on the answer sheets.

Both authors of this article were present when instructions were given. The students were told they could write the answers in Finnish, English or French.

Table 1: Respondents' associations before and after receiving additional information (N=42).

	BEFORE		AFTER	
	n	(%)	n	(%)
Coffee related	23	(14.2)	6	(4.8)
Advertisement (statement)	14	(8.6)	10	(8.0)
Advertisement (critical)	1	(0.6)	4	(3.2)
Nature related:	40	(24.7)	2	(1.6)
southern nature	20		1	
extraordinary natural phenomenon	9		-	
other nature related	11		1	
Beauty/naturalness	7	(4.3)	2	(1.6)
Colour	7	(4.3)	8	(6.4)
Object (other than coffee bean)	9	(5.6)	-	
Human being related:	25	(15.4)	15	(12.0)
woman	8		4	
man	2		-	
black person	2		3	
female genitalia	5		2	
other body parts	4		2	
other human related	4		4	
Sexuality	2	(1.2)	2	(1.6)
Feeling, atmosphere	1	(0.6)	2	(1.6)
Exploitation/oppression:	17	(10.5)	32	(25.6)
exploitation & slavery	3		5	
violence	6		10	
human being as an object	3		8	
bad feeling	2		3	
humble position	2		2	
developing countries/the	1		4	

world				
Contemplative	2	(1.2)	1	(0.8)
Offensive:	1	(0.6)	14	(11.2)
racist	-		5	
sexist	-		8	
offensive	1		1	
Non-offensive:	1	(0.6)	17	(13.6)
non-racist	-		9	
non-sexist	-		7	
non-offensive	1		1	
Both (offensive and non-offensive)	-		2	(1.6)
Other	12	(7.4)	8	(6.4)
Total	162	(99.8 %)	125	(100 %)
Total of responses	42			42
Missing responses	-			5

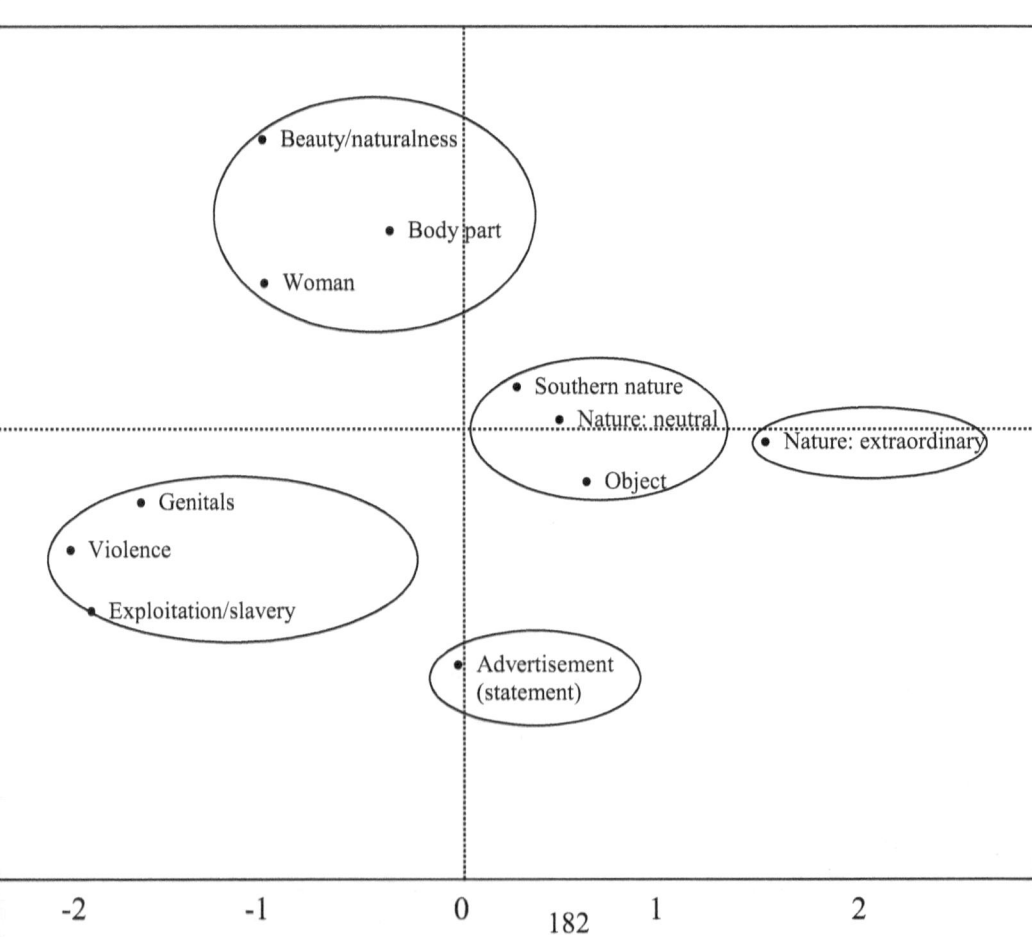

The results

Immediate images and associations

The answers the respondents gave can be seen in Table 1. The category of coffee related imagery includes among others words such as "coffee bean", "a coffee shop", and "a coffee-person". The category of southern nature imagery includes among others "warmth", "from the deep south" and "the sun is shining", the category of other nature related imagery includes among others "a clam", "a caterpillar" and "clouds". The category of violence includes among others "rape", "humiliating" and "abused". The respondents had a total of 162 associations before receiving additional information and 125 associations afterwards. Every single association was categorized and therefore a respondent may have more than one association in one category.

As Table 1 illustrates, different associations relating to nature were very common in the first round of answers. There were also a lot of answers relating to a human being and coffee. The second most common category was oppression/violence.

In order to analyze the structure of the body of answers we conducted a correspondence analysis on the answers gathered in the first round with the SPAD-t program developed for processing textual data. (see e.g. Lebart, Morineau, Becue & Hacusler, 1993). In this analysis we included all categories of association that had a minimum frequency of three after overlap on the level of an individual respondent had been removed. Category of association refers to the subcategories mentioned in Table 1, or the main category if there are no subcategories. Category "other" has been excluded, as well as the category "a man", the contribution of which would be 100 per cent in the correspondence analysis.

Table 1 illustrates the location of all those categories that had a value higher than the average (i.e. more than 6.2) on the first two dimensions. These dimensions explain 26.6 per cent of the overall variation detected. Figure 1 shows that the first dimension mostly divides the nature related associations from others. The second dimension can be described as separating positive beauty estimates and other answers.

A cluster analysis of the categories defined the comprehensive picture of the answers. In our five-cluster approach the first group includes the categories of "southern nature", "neutral nature" and "objects". The second group consists of "extraordinary nature", and the third group of "advertisement: statement". The fourth group includes "woman", "other body parts" and "beauty/naturalness". The fifth group includes "female genitalia", "oppression/slavery" and "violence".

As stated above, Figure 1 shows only the categories that had a contribution above average. Therefore, for example categories "coffee related" and "advertisement as a piece of art" are included in the fourth group, but are not shown in the figure. The fifth cluster includes the category of "a human being as an object" as well.

Changes caused by receiving additional information

The answers gathered in the second round cannot be directly compared with those of the first round. It can be assumed that the respondents mostly wrote down any new kinds of associations they had in the second round. On the other hand, they may also have continued along the same lines as in the first round if they had some more similar associations.

Overall, there was a significantly lesser amount of associations related to coffee and nature in the second round, which is probably explained by the fact that they were already common in the first round. There were more associations relating to exploitation and violence and they now formed the largest category. A quarter of all answers fell into this category. It is clear that some of the respondents made new interpretations of the picture after they received additional information, perceived different things in the picture than before, and for some of the respondents receiving the information made interpretations of exploitation and violence possible. One fifth of the respondents commented on the picture on an axis of offensive/non-offensive. Comments that it was non-offensive were somewhat more frequent than comments of offensiveness. In other words, the respondents also offered views that were in contrast to the given frame of reference. The sparse amount of data does not allow examining the mental imagery of the respondents who described the picture either as offensive or non-offensive separately.

The uneven sex distribution of the respondents makes examining the data in regard to gender impossible. The only thing that can be said based on the results is that the answers are not clearly divided into male and female associations and images.

Discussion

Our respondents were select, university students in the capital city, but they were not a group specialized in discrimination and gender equality questions in particular. It can therefore be assumed that they had no access to the information and categorization methods of experts in this area when they were answering our questions. Nevertheless, students are usually interested in current social topics, which can be considered positive in regard to the formulation of our study question. Their responses therefore do not represent the average of the population nor those of experts, they are more representative of the associations so-called enlightened laypersons may have. This type of persons may be considered an ideal group of respondents when examining the limits of what is and is not allowed, what is and is not offensive in a society.

Beauty and violence
When we evaluate all we have presented above as a comprehensive whole, we can draw the conclusion that the advertisement for *Café Arome* has been discussed in public arenas in a very one-sided manner. The comments quoted in the weekly supplement of *Helsingin Sanomat*, including that of the Consumer Ombudsman, overlapped with only one of the five categories that emerged when examining the responses of the students: the category which included "woman", "body parts other than genitalia", "beauty-naturalness" and "advertisement as a piece of art". It is worth noticing that neither the men who commented on the advertisement in the newspaper supplement nor the Council of Ethics in Advertising brought up anything clearly related to sexuality and violence such as the students did.

Nevertheless, it is clear that the advertisement inspires many kinds of associations and mental images and some of them make the fact that many felt the advertisement is offensive or oppressive understandable. One of our respondents had the association of a black female slave who is ready to fulfill sexual desires ("a submitting black female slave, ready to be enjoyed"). Another respondent said "the woman portrays a coffee bean naked; she is something to be enjoyed in a humble position, ready for your desires". A quarter of the respondents made references to exploitation and violence in the first round of answers. In the second round, the racist and sexist frame of reference we offered brought up some more responses of exploitation and violence. Some of the respondents saw things in the picture that were new to them after receiving additional information. It is impossible to say exactly how many of the respondents gave their answers according to what they assumed we wanted to hear. The additional information did not in any case serve to lead all students to make associations accordingly, for some of the respondents explicitly said they thought the advertisement was not offensive. Naturally, it is also possible that a person may have seen violence in the picture but did not consider it offensive. What is most remarkable and noteworthy about the responses is that along with the aesthetic there were also clearly negative themes, that after receiving additional information the respondents gave more of these types of answers, and that there were divergent answers regarding the offensiveness of the picture.

From a social psychological viewpoint the results are not surprising. We have long had information on how our folk theories, i.e. social representations, are constructed in layers utilizing our historical sphere of experience (e.g. Moscovici, 1984, de Rosa 1987). This idea has been reinforced by the experimental studies on stereotypes and prejudice (e.g. Devine, 1989). Within the sphere of women's studies the way women of colonial countries are depicted and objectified in Western art has been analyzed very illustratively (e.g. Rantonen, summary [1999]). Based on research data we know that our sphere of experience today is influenced by historical events. Our mental imagery is profuse.

Advertising, on the other hand, knowingly makes use of mental imagery. According to an everyday idea prevalent in the world of science, a lot of money is put into advertising and its design. How are we to understand the *Café Arome* advertisement against this background? Were the designers of the advert unaware of the themes of violence and sexuality that the advertisement, based on our findings, inspires? Or did they knowingly take advantage of this very fact? The goal of this article is not to answer either of these questions.

Instead, our goal is to prove that the *Café Arome* advertisement should be seen as ambiguous when evaluating it. There is no denying that it is easy to see it as beautiful, but at the same time we have to admit that it also inspires the kind of images which are critical when evaluating the acceptability of the advertisement.

Our respondents formed a small, select group of white, young, European people. Above we have discussed why their responses in particular are nevertheless interesting in regard to the formulation of the study question in this article. The persons who gave them instructions have very different skin pigmentations and coming face to face with people of different skin colours is a part of everyday life in Finland today. Therefore, although our results cannot be statistically generalized to apply to all Finns and it is probable that matters relating to the circumstances of the research situation have some effect on the results (as they always do), the results cannot be discredited on these grounds. They prove that in previous evaluations of the advertisement, both in the contexts of judicial matters and the advertising community, the mental imagery it inspires has been discussed too one-sidedly. The ways of interpreting the advertisement that are more relevant in evaluating offensiveness and oppressiveness which, based on our study, are entirely possible, have been completely excluded from public discussion.

Discrimination, offensiveness and justifications

The Council of Ethics in Advertising has handled the *Café Arome* advertisement from the point of view of racial and gender discrimination. The statement notes that nudity is not offensive in itself. One of our respondents had a similar association, he said of the advertisement: "Not at all [offending]…the focus isn't on her breasts etc." In terms of social representations we can say that in our society, inviolate gender equality is anchored to the naked breasts of a woman. However, in public discussion these over-simplifying categorizations should be overcome and a more detailed understanding of these matters reached. Therefore we propose that noting the ambiguity of the *Café Arome* advertisement and interpreting it in regard to inviolate human dignity would have been essential in discussing it publicly and making decisions on it.

What is interesting in the Council's statement is that it mentions offensiveness, not only discrimination. This compares with the ruling of the Market Court discussed earlier. Therefore, it seems obvious that our society is ready to use such criteria as "human dignity" and "offence" when evaluating advertisements. Discussion on how these things are evaluated is, on the other hand, rare. Previously we have said (Kassea & Pirttilä-Backman, 1999) that it may be an unreasonable demand for everyone to be able to effectively specify factors that influence gender equality in the context of different kinds of interventions. We then proposed that sufficient sensitivity and the skill to analyze should be ensured at least on the level of teams and working groups in a professional context. Accordingly, we propose that teams with sufficient abilities to widely understand the imagery of Finnish society be used in evaluating advertisements. Only then can we have justified discussion on what is offensive in advertisements in the 21st century.

A counterargument to the more varied discussion we proposed above could be that the sphere of imagery (with its historical dimension) is too difficult to include, that the borders are thin lines which can be discussed until the end of time. It is true that we will discuss these things forever because history, culture and humanity's understanding of itself change constantly. However, this does not indicate that the human being is not a creature of history and culture and that these dimensions should be ignored. In this context it is furthermore interesting to notice that the law on radio and television prohibits the use of subliminal visual and audio elements. Although the ambiguity of mental images is a more difficult matter to deal with than subliminal advertising this does not mean it could be ignored. It is also interesting to notice that advertisers explicitly concede the impact of mental imagery in another context, as we can see in the following.

Article 5 of the regulations discussed above states that:

"1. Advertisements should not contain any statement or visual presentation which *directly or by implication, omission, ambiguity or exaggerated claim* (italics by authors) is likely to mislead the consumer, in particular with regard to

a) characteristics such as: nature, composition, method and date of manufacture, range of use, efficiency and performance, quantity, commercial or geographical origin or environmental impact;

b) the value of the product and the total price actually to be paid;

c) delivery, exchange, return, repair and maintenance;

d) terms of guarantee;

e) copyright and industrial property rights such as patents, trademarks, designs and models and trade names;

f) official recognition or approval, awards such as medals, prizes and diplomas;

g) the extent of benefits for charitable causes.

Advertisements should not misuse research results or quotations from technical and scientific publications. Statistics should not be so presented as to exaggerate the validity of advertising claims. Scientific terms should not be used to falsely ascribe scientific validity to advertising claims."

Furthermore, according to Article 7 "advertisements should not denigrate any firm, organization, industrial or commercial activity, profession or product by seeking to bring it or them into public contempt or ridicule, or in any similar way."[12]

The above can be interpreted to mean that human beings may be demeaned and caused to experience anxiety, but products and organizations should be protected. Considering the matters brought up in this article this conclusion is not, however, justified. Nevertheless, there seems to be a sore need for discussion on the criteria of

---

[12] Translator's note: in the ICC Consolidated Code of Marketing and Advertising Communication Practice published in 2006 this has been amended to include persons: "Marketing communication should not denigrate any person or group of persons, firm, organisation, industrial or commercial activity, profession or product, or seek to bring it or them into public contempt or ridicule."

offensiveness and discrimination as well as the content of legislation and other regulations.

References

The Council for Ethics in Advertising, The Central Chamber of Commerce in Finland. Statement on April 27th, 1999.

de Rosa, A. (1987). "The social representations of mental illness in children and adults." In W. Doise and S. Moscovici (Eds.), *Current Issues in European Social psychology*, Vol. 2, 47–138. Cambridge: Cambridge University Press.

Devine, P.G. (1989). "Stereotypes and prejudice: Their automatic and controlled components." *Journal of personality and Social Psychology*, 56, 5–18.

Finland's third periodic report on the implementation of the Convention on the Elimination of All Forms of Discrimination against Women, UN. (1997). *Publications of the Ministry of Foreign Affairs* 6.

Heinonen, V. (1999). Comment. *Helsingin Sanomat weekly supplement NYT*, No 3, p. 41.

Kassea, B. R. and Pirttilä-Backman, A-M. (1999). *Gender equality in the Finnish African development co-operations projects*. Ministry of Foreign Affairs, Blue series, 2.

Konttinen, H. (1999). Comment. *Helsingin Sanomat weekly supplement NYT*, No 3, p. 41.

Lebart, L., Morineau, A., Becuem M. and Haeusler, L. (1993). *Spad-t. Systéme Portable d'Analyse de Données Textuelles*. Saint-Mandé: CISIA.

International Chamber of Commerce. (1997). *Mainonnan kansainväliset perussäännöt*. [ICC International Code of Advertising Practice.]

International Chamber of Commerce. (2006). *Consolidated ICC Code of Advertising and Market Communication Practice*.

Mickwitz, E. (1999). Comment. *Helsingin Sanomat weekly supplement NYT*, No 3, p. 41.

Miles, R. (1994). *Rasismi*. (A. Tiusanen and J. Koivisto, Trans.) Tampere: Vastapaino (original *Racism* published 1989).

Moscovici, S. (1984). "The phenomenon of social representations." In R. Farr and S. Moscovici (Eds.), *Social representations* (pp. 181–209). London: Cambridge University Press.

Rantonen, E. (1999). "Lansimaisten kuvien rotunaiset." [Western images of ethnic women.] In J. Airaksinen and T. Ripatti (Eds.), *Rotunaisia ja feminismejä* [Ethnic women and feminisms] (pp. 41–62). Tampere: Vastapaino.

Scheinin, M. (1996). "Mitä on syrjintä?" [What is discrimination?] In T. Dahlgren, J. Kortteinen, K.J. Lång, M. Pentikäinen and M. Scheinin (Eds.), *Vähemmistöt ja niiden syrjintä Suomessa* [Minorities and discrimination in Finland.] (pp. 7–19). Helsinki: Yliopistopaino.

Gender Representation In Religious Discourse In Nigeria

Akin Odebunmi
University of Ibadan, Nigeria

Introduction

Gender and religion strike a lot in common. This is because religious roles are largely earmarked on the basis of gender differences and assumed capabilities of members of the genders by societies. Leadership roles, for example, in many religions are reserved for men, while other roles are largely retained for women, a situation that is quite evident in the Christian religion. While the situation is changing in some parts of the world, the status quo has remained in some others. It is against this background that this paper examines how gender is represented in the language of Christian religious expression in Nigeria. To address the issue correctly, it is essential to devote some attention to the concept of gender per se.

"Gender, in broad terms, refers to the sex-role identity used by humans to emphasise the distinctions between males and females" (Adegbite, 2009:12). It differs from sex in that while sex works with biological and physical features of humans, gender is social and relates to roles and behaviours performed by sexes (Lamidi 2009). Research in gender-bound language has, therefore, focused on the wary gender comes into communication and how this has influenced the structure and functions of language in general. It has shown how language is drawn upon to construct and come to terms with the semantics and identities of personal, social and cultural dimensions (cf Yusuf 1988, 1993,1997a; Adegbite 2009).

As would be established, existing studies in gender linguistics have focused on the differences and similarities between male and female linguistic expressions in general and specific terms across several domains. They have also considered how power, race and class have influenced gendered language (Mills 2003). Except in the West and north Africa (see Walsh 2002; Jule 2006; Sadiqi 2003), the studies have however not attended seriously to how gender is expressed in religions, especially Christianity, from strictly linguistic perspectives. Much of what has obtained hitherto have been studies with sociological and anthropological orientations. The other dimension has been the concern about the language of religion in general with reference to Christianity without any specific attention given to the gender aspect in Africa and Nigeria in particular. These are gaps that should be filled as the sociological and anthropological studies cannot provide a full x- ray of the gender picture in religious discourses. It is essential to determine the linguistic tools drawn upon in the Christian religion, and the possible influence of the institution on the choices made. The paper thus has the ambition to illuminate the gender linguistic and discoursal resources engaged in religious expression in Nigeria and clarify, to some extent, the state of gender theorizing in religious discourse in the country.

Methodology and Design

Two religious institutions, namely, The Nigerian Baptist Theological Seminary, Ogbomoso and the Dominican Institute, Ibadan, representing the Baptist and Catholic denominations (both being orthodox churches) were purposively sampled. The two institutions offered degrees in Theology (and philosophy), and were, therefore, considered appropriate for the data needed for the study as the students were advanced ones who had largely formed their own opinions about issues and were capable of some level of critical thinking. At different times, each of the Use of English classes of the institutions (where I teach as an adjunct lecturer) was subjected to a spontaneous writing exercise on "God and Humans". A total of 78 essays were collected. These were subjected to linguistic and pragma-discoursal analyses. Insights were particularly deployed from gender theories, discourse tracking and critical discourse analysis. In the next section (i.e. 3), I review gender and theo-religious discourse. In section 4, I establish theoretical perspectives within which the data is housed. In section 5, I review studies on gender and religion. In Section 6, I review gender theories. In Section 7, I analyze the data and present my findings. In section 8, I conclude the paper.

Gender Linguistics and Theo-Religious Discourse

Gender linguistics refers to the study of language elements that point to human sexes. This however does not work perfectly within the traditional grammatical concept of gender. According to Corbett (1991:1),

To understand what linguists mean by 'gender', a good starting point is Hockett's definition: 'Genders are classes of nouns reflected in the behaviour of associated words' (1958:231). A language may have two or more such classes of genders. The classification frequently corresponds to a real-world distinction of sex, at least in part, but often too it does not ('gender' derives etymologically from Latin *genus*, via Old French *gendre*, and originally meant 'kind' or 'sort'). The word 'gender' is not used for just a group of nouns but also for the whole category; thus we may say that a particular language has, say, three genders, masculine, feminine and neuter, and that the language has the category of gender.

The three genders, masculine, feminine and neuter, are represented in English through nouns and pronouns. These include, respectively, "man" (his, him), "woman" (her, hers), "animal" (it). However, there are many words in English that do not fit with the genders, especially the masculine and the feminine. These words, in the pre-feminist linguistic movement period were associated with the masculine gender, e.g. doctor (his), engineer (his), etc. The situation has however changed with the revolution brought in by feminist linguistics which has introduced many gender-balanced and gender-neutral elements into the English language (see for example Deborah Cameron and her research). These changes are largely reflected in anaphoric pronominal reference. Partitive pronouns such as "everybody", "somebody", "anybody", etc no longer take the masculine anaphor "his", but rather his/her or her/his, depending on the perspective and stance of the writer. The singular 'they' has also been introduced to neutralise the genderisation of common nouns such as "doctor", "student", "engineer", etc. This pronoun is also applicable to partitive pronouns.

Changes have also occurred with respect to genderised nouns such as "man", "chairman", etc which have respectively been neutralised as "man and woman", "humans or human"; and "chairperson". Maxims such as "man proposes, God disposes" have become altered as "To propose is human, to dispose divine" (Yusuf1997b). This is the point where religious discourse becomes influenced by developments in feminist linguistics. The problem with the original (former) expression is its patriarchal posture which presents the man as subsuming the woman. Scholars (Grohman 1998) of religions such as Christianity, Buddhism, Judaism and Islam, who are not favourably disposed to the patriarchal order that rules the religions and who have converged under the aegis of feminist theology have challenged this order, and have proposed balanced linguistic and discourse tools to handle the biases in the religions. The goals of feminist theology, therefore, includes: raising the level of the role women play in the clerical circle, revising the patriarchal image and language attached to God in the religions, placing women appropriately in the religions' concepts of career and motherhood, and investigating the portrayal of women in the scriptural texts (Grohman 1998; *Encyclopaedia of Science and Religion*, 2009; Cline 2009).

The present research is particularly concerned about the feminist theologist's revision of the language used in reference to God and dominant patriarchal influence on Christianity. This interest immediately necessitates the inclusion of ideology in the framework for handling the data. This consideration is taken together with the choice of discourse tracking which explains the network of reference items that are engaged to refer to God and describe the genders. Thus, in the next section, I review briefly tracking and ideology.

Theoretical Perspectives: Discourse Tracking And Ideology

Odebunmi (2008:81) defines tracking as "the linguistic and discoursal means by which connections are maintained between different parts of texts to enhance the sense-making process of the texts". This means that tracking incorporates all the devices employed in a text to ensure textuality and comprehension.

Martin and Rose (2003) identify four types of tracking resources. These are presenting, presuming, possessive and comparative.

Presenting devices introduce discourse items, which are, subsequently, referred to by presuming devices. Possessive resources mark off possession while comparative ones point out the relationships between propositions and discourse items. One point to note, however, is that all the four resources can be subsumed, in functional terms, under the presenting and presuming frames. In these frames, the following devices are engaged: anaphora, bridging, cataphora, esphora, homophora and exophora. Anaphora makes reference to the back, e.g. "Professor Davidson is tall. *He* is also handsome". Bridging connects a presenting discourse item indirectly, e.g. "The Independent Electoral Commission took the lead *The Commission* was commended for its efforts". Cataphoric reference goes forwards, e.g. "Here is *the news:* a suicide bomber was caught in Lagos". Esphoric reference goes forward within a single frame, e.g. "The plea *of the accused*". Homophora moves outside the text on the basis of common grounds shared between interactants e.g. "*The* International Legal Commission". Exophoric reference picks items outside the text; e.g. "*We* shall do our best to save his life, the doctor said":

As Odebunmi (2008) argues, tracking has a high ideological value for the proposition tracked, and the tracking devices drawn upon are often based in certain institutionalised beliefs. Thus ideology is defined as "implicit assumptions held, largely in interaction with power relations" (Odebunmi 2008:81 [Fairclough 2001, Wodak 1996]). Odebunmi states further that it is in this implicitness that lies the capacity of ideology to give sustenance to power inequalities and thus serve "political purposes" (2008:81). In a related manner, placing ideology in Critical Discourse Analysis (CDA) where it has always resided, Wodak (2007:209) submits:

Ideology, for CDA, is seen as an important means of establishing and maintaining unequal power relations. CDA takes a particular interest in the ways in which language mediates ideology in a variety of social institutions.

In the same vein, Fairclough (2003: 9) observes that ideology relates to "representations of aspects of the world which can be shown to contribute to establishing, maintaining and changing of social relations of power, dominations ans exploitation". This is done "very subtly, but sometimes overtly" (Atanga 2009: [van Dijk 1998, 2007; Reisigl and Wodak 2001; Fairclough 2001, 2003; Blommaert 2005).

The fact that ideology resides in social groups makes it institutional and is therefore beyond the individual. In the words of Wodak and Weiss (2003:14), ideology covers

> Social reforms and processes within which and by means of which, symbolic forms circulate in the social world... there are specific historical reasons why people come to feel, reason, desire and imagine as they do

This position points to the fact that genders, races, classes, and groups have ideologies which influence their perspectives and horizons. Thus, the Christian religion as a social institution does not escape the grip of ideology which reflects in its patriarchal framing and orientation, and which has consequently attracted criticisms and reactions from feminist theologians as stated earlier. It is therefore interesting to investigate how gender ideology manifests in the theological environment and or religious discourse in Nigeria. Meanwhile, I provide a brief review of studies on gender and religion below

Studies on Gender and Religion

Gender and religion have received good attention in the literature. However, much of the studies in this direction has come from the sociological, anthropological and theological perspectives. Gallagher and Smith (1999) evaluate the degree of the challenge posed to institutionalized masculinity by modern evangelical standards. They observe that what holds sway, to a great extent, among the evangelicals is a situation-driven relation of equality between men and women. In another paper on evangelicals, Gallagher (2004) looks at the position of conservative protestants to feminism. He finds out that, to the protestant, feminism has no religious or political influence.

Wolkomier (2004) investigates how Christian women who are conservatives negotiate identities in the gay spousal context. He finds out that the women in this condition simply hang on to divine support. Adams (2009) explores the prohibition of women from holding leadership positions in the church. Avishai (2008) moves beyond the literature that interrogates women's complicity and considers the agency of religious women as a conduct within the precincts of religious practice.

Read (2000) examines the conflicts that emerge in terms of the meanings associated with veiling among the elite who are Muslims and Muslims who are feminists. He investigates how the conflicts bear on the negotiation of identity among Muslim women who veil and those who do not. The Tijaniyya group in Kano, Nigeria, is studied by Huston (2001) in terms of the manifestation of the patriarchal order in the group. The paper shows that the women in high spiritual positions in the group submit to the group's patriarchy while still exhibiting some level of independence.

In the literary axis, Causey (2009) reviews Ania Loomba's book, *Shakespeare, Race and Colonialism* in which the author (Loomba) discusses the space allocated to women in the Shakespearean play, *Othello,* and the link this establishes with men and religion. This focus, like the rest of the others already reviewed, immediately sets the present study from the existing ones on gender and religion. It is thus clear that rare are the studies that have addressed gender representation in religious discourse. In the main, this study is charting a path in the linguistic investigation of the feminist theologians' impacts on religious discourse in Nigeria and examining the extent to which the language of religious expression has sustained or devalued institutional patriarchy in Christianity. In the next section, I briefly review gender theories.

Gender Theories

Gender theories have been approached from two angles: binary and non-binary. The binary angle bifurcates into dominance and differences approaches while the non-binary one considers gender, as a construction, on a domain and specific basis. First I, consider the binary approach.

Binary Theories of Gender

Each of dominance and difference approaches is considered briefly here. First, I take the dominance theory. Through what Lakoff (1975:10) dubs, "talking like a lady", she describes the way male dominance over the female reflects in language use. This path was one of the earliest ones followed in gender research in the 1970s where the issue of male dominance and female subservience was considered (Lakoff 1975; Spender 1980).

The dominance patterns established as features of women's language are presented as follows:

1. Lexical hedges e.g. you know, sort of ...
2. Tag question e.g. she is very nice, isn't she?
3. Rising intonation and declaratives, e.g. It's really good
4. Empty adjectives e.g. divine, charming, etc
5. Precise colour terms, e.g. magenta, acqamarine
6. intensifiers such as *just* and *so*
7. Hypercorrect grammar, e.g. consistent use of standard verb forms
8. Superpolite forms, e.g. indirect requests, euphemisms
9. Avoidance of strong swears words, e.g. fudge, my goodness
10. Emphatic stress, e.g. it was a BRILLIANT performance

(Holmes 1993:314[Lakoff 1975])

These features have been seen by early feminist scholars as indices of women's subordinateness to men and the latter's powerfulness. Yet much as these theorists have been able to challenge some dominance tendencies among certain groups of men, they have been criticised for being narrow in scope and for not being representative in terms of the totality of all women's linguistic behaviours.

The difference theorists, on the other hand, do not see the language of men and women as reflecting tendencies of dominant and dominated groups. Rather, they "turned to an analysis of the socially constructed differences between women's and men's language, seeing these as akin to dialects spoken by different groups who interacted with each other" (Mills, 2003:166). Tannen (1991) contends that women's language should essentially differ from men's because the two undergo different socialisation processes in which they are made to opt for different styles of language. She further argues that the two genders go into conversational interactions with different interests: men are interested in "rapport talk" while men are interested in "report talk" (cf Mills 2003: 166).

Ambitious as the stance of the difference theorists sounds, it has been flawed on the ground that it is politically reactionary and that it is blind to the asymmetry common in men/women relations (cf Troemel-Ploetz, 1998). Cameron (1998) also decries the absence of power relations in the theoretical conception of gender by difference theorists, a feature that she considers quintessential in the interactions between men and women.

Non-Binary Theory

The non-binary theory of gender emanates from the criticisms of both approaches in the binary class. The non-binary approach is thus shifted away from the overgeneralising and dichotomysing stances of the binary group. Theorists in this group are interested in making
more nuanced and mitigated statements about certain groups of women or men in particular circumstances, who reaffirm, negotiate with, and challenge the parameters of permissible or socially sanctioned behaviour (Mills 2003: 169-170.

Some studies in this direction include Cameron and Coates (1988), Johnson and Meinhoff (1997), Bing and Bergall (1996), Witing (1992) and Queen (1997). These theorists have examined, in pragmatic terms, linguistic relations and identity representations among men and women in different communities and among different groups such as miners, racial groups and lesbians.

It is interesting to note that much as the dominance approach seems to have been battered on the grounds already highlighted, it is found the most relevant to the data in the present study. This will be shown clearly in the analysis that follows. This paper, therefore, largely taps into the posture of unequal power relations which dominance theorists expose and which synchronise with the principles of critical discourse analysis.

Analysis and Findings

As stated in Section 2, 78 essays, all of which were analysed for gender elements, were collected from the two institutions sampled. Seventy two (72) of these were males while six (6) were females. The analysis of the data is both quantitative and qualitative

The data reveal that two gender-related terms recur in the written discourse of theological students in Nigeria, namely, patriarchal terms

and gender – neutral/ balanced terms. The realisations of these terms are tested against the tenets of feminist theologists, which:
  i. reject the notion that God has a male gender
  ii. do not encourage the use of male pronouns to refer to God

It is further determined if the data exhibit balanced or biased perspectives on the genders' representation of humanity. Each of the terms identified is now taken in turn.

Patriarchal Terms

The patriarchal terms observed in the discourse are considered in terms of those used with reference to God and those used in relation to human beings as males or females. I consider each below.

God in the Patriarchal Picture

Five items are associated with God in the discourse: God, Father, He, His and Him. Details of the realisations are presented in the chart below:

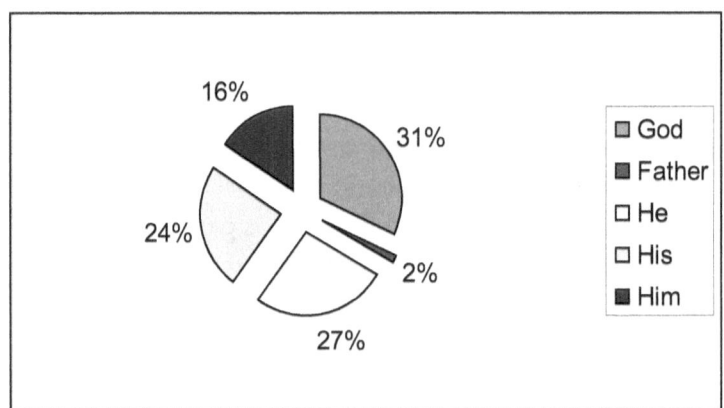

Figure 1: "God" and Patriarchy

Figure I shows that with 31%, 'God' takes predominance over 'He' (with 27%), which, in the data, tracks it anaphorically. 'His', a variant of 'He' (with 24%) follows 'He'. This is followed by 'him', (with 16%), another pronominal variant of "He". 'Father' takes the least percentage (2%).

The subjects do not consider an alternative for 'God' despite the teachings of feminist theologists which are aimed at providing alternative terms. One expects the altercative to be, at least, reflected in the pronominal variants, especially if God is considered a neutral term. This does not occur as the population either repeat 'God' across their essays or replace 'God' with patriarchal variants "He", "His" and "Him". "Father" is however not as frequently used as these pronominal items. The pragmatics of this low representation would emerge by and by.

It is essential to consider how the genders represent the terms. The table below provides the information:

Table 1: Male and Female Representation of "God".

Variable: God	Male = 72	Female = 6	Total	%
God	72	6	78	40.84
Father	01	03	04	2.09
He	60	05	11	5.76
His	57	03	60	31.41
Him	36	02	38	19.90
	226	19	191	100

Table 1 shows the variation in the realisation of 'God' by the genders. Percentage scores of the each gender are more revealing:

Table 2: Female Representation of "God".

Variable	Gender	Items	Frequency	%
God	Feminine	God	6	31.58
		Father	3	15.79
		He	5	26.32
		His	3	15.79
		Him	2	10.53
		Total	19	100

Table 3: Male Representation of "God".

Variable	Gender	Items	Frequency	%
God	Masculine	God	72	31.86
		Father	01	0.44
		He	60	26.55
		His	57	25.22
		Him	36	15.93
		Total	226	100

From tables 2 and 3, it is shown that there is hardly any obvious difference between the way the genders realise the items "God", "he" and "him". There is however a clear difference in the realization of 'Father'. With 3 out of the six subjects (15.79 overall; 50% on a single sex (female) basis)) opting for father among the feminine gender and 1 out of 72 selecting same (0.4) among the masculine gender, a serious ideological implication emerges. The principle of dominance and subservience obviously comes into play. This goes in accordance with the African Gender ideologies (Atanga 2009). The men, already playing the social role of "father" are not instinctively drawn to the choice of the word, but the women, admitting the superiority of men, see God as "father". This becomes interesting in the light of current trends in spousal discourse in Nigeria, especially in Southwestern Nigeria, where the research took place. I have personally observed that husbands are generally referred to as "our daddy" (our father) by about 85% of the Christian married women. This phenomenon is thus tracked in operation by the prospective (Christian) female pastors, some of whom are not even married.

The subservience shown in the choice of "father" by the feminine gender again defeats the stance of feminine theologists regarding both the use of non- patriarchal terms for "God", and the encouragement of neutral terms to describe the Almighty God. This then speaks of the institutionalization of male dominance in the mainstream theology which precedes feminist theology, and which is the major focus of the theological schools studied. The ideology could also be traced to the culture of the Southwestern Nigeria, and to a large extent Nigeria as a whole (and to a great extent, Africa in general), which places the man at the head point and makes the woman to submit to him, the same stance that has spurred feminist theology.

Men and Women in the Patriarchal Picture

The discourse presents only two items here: "mankind" and "man".

Table 4 shows the distribution across the data:

Variable	Items	Frequency	%
Men and women	Mankind	3	4.84
	Man	59	95.16
	Total	62	100.00

Table 4 shows that "man" occurs in about 95.16% compared to "mankind" which occurs in about 4.84% in the patriarchal perspective. This shows that both genders prefer the term "man" to "mankind", perhaps for the Christian institutional ideology and Nigerian cultural intervention already discussed above. It is, however, interesting to move beyond this general picture to see how each gender considers the items. Details are found in Table 5 below:

Table 5: Genders' Realisations of "Mankind" and "Man"

Variable "Men and women"	Mankind	Man	Total
Male	3 (5.2%)	55 (94.8%)	58
Female	0	04 (100%)	04

The table shows that men use the term "man" more frequently than women do, but they use "mankind" not a frequently as they do "man". Women, on their own part, in the two institutions, do not draw on "mankind" at all. The comparison of the uses would emerge from the next two tables where each gender's employment is taken in its own right:

Table 5 presents interesting findings by showing that:
i. more women than men employ "man"
ii. only a small number of men use "mankind"
iii. No woman uses "mankind"

We can deduce from these findings that the dominance of the patriarchal order still accounts for the predominant use of "man", especially by the women, who prefer it to "mankind" which they largely replace with other plural forms as will be shown later. The argument that the subjects, including the male, consider "mankind" as an overtly plural form, when compared to "man", applies across the data. Hence, many of the men also avoid it, opting for the clearer and superior "man".

It is interesting to note that many of the men assert the superiority of their gender by their use of "man" as against the use to which women put the item. An example follows:

> Ex. 1:
> Man, representing humans, has
> seen that humans have
> dual values – the physical
> nature and the divine nature.

This claim "man representing humans" does not just dwell on the generic knowledge of "man"; it touches also on the socio-cultural conception that a woman is subordinate to a man. This is more so in the context of Christianity, in which the population operate, where Paul has stated that women should be silent in the church, on order which has permeated the Christendom especially in Nigeria, despite the intervention of feminist theology.

Women, on the other hand, use "man" in an objective manner, while still referring to both genders. The following example explains this point:

> Ex.2
> Man committed sin and became
> sinners in the sight of God, [sic]
> that was how the relationship broke.

The woman-subject here submits to the patriarchal order by allowing her gender to be carried along with that of the man. She sees herself as a part of the man, a teaching which Christianity and its theology advance.

As earlier hinted, "mankind" is treated as a plural form. Hence, many of the subjects opt for other alternatives. The following shows this:

Ex.3
God is the final judge of the [sic]
mankind that is human [sic] are
responsible to unlike other creatures [sic]

In this example, the male subject chooses a nominal rather than a pronominal item to make the required anaphoric reference as he is not sure if 'they' would fit into the context. This applies in a large number of cases.

Gender–Neural and Gender- Balanced Items

The data do not reveal any gender neutral item for God. There are however a few items engaged with respect to men and women. Some of these are nominal while some are pronominal in form. Their occurrences are presented in the table below:

Table 6: Men, Women and Gender Neutral/balanced Items

Variable	Item	Frequency	Percentage
Men and women	Humankind	02	1.02
	The people	08	4.08
	Humanity	09	4.59
	Male and female	11	5.61
	Human being	34	17.35
	All people	06	3.06
	Humans	68	34.69
	Everyone/anyone his/her, him/her	28	14.29
	Us	08	4.08
	We	22	11.22
	Total	196	100

Table 6 presents both gender-neutral ("humankind", "the people", "humanity", "human beings", "all people", "humans", "us" and "we") and gender-balanced ("male/female", "man/woman", "everyone/anyone/his/her", "him/her") items. The higher percentage carried by humans could be attributed to the inclusion of the item in the topic of the essay examined. Hence, about 68 out of the 78 subjects use it. Apart from that, it provides a tool of pluralisation which patriarchal items such as "mankind" do not have. Hence, in most instances where the plural form for the patriarchal "man" or other singular–masculine items is required, the default choice is "humans" or "human beings" which comes next to it in distribution. One example can be cited here:

> Ex.5
> God created man in His own
> image in order for them [sic] to
> oversees [sic] all the creation [sic]
> God made or created. Human beings
> were the result of the sixth day of
> creation in the diary of God.

Here, "human being" preempted in the first sentence as "them" (mistaken for the plural form of 'man' in anaphoric relations) comes in as the plural form of "man" where the male-subject here intends to refer to "all people".

Other gender-neutral or gender – balanced items are used as presenting or presuming elements to track "human" in the essays. Hence, their realisations vary according to the preference of the writer. The following example presents a good demonstration of the tracking pattern of the items.

> Ex.7
> Evil found its root in the
> disobedience of Adam and Eve.
> Since then, ***man*** has had to
> struggle and sweat to get ***his***
> daily bread. God in his mercy
> despite man's disobedience still
> bestows blessings on ***him***. Man
> also recognises God's tender
> love. When God blesses ***him,***
> he smiles and says 'Thank God'.
> ***Some*** even go as far as
> crying. This happens when ***someone*** is
> at the climax of his happiness ….

Across the extract here, many alternatives are provided for "man", which begins from the proper nouns "Adam" and "Eve". The male subject here does not see the male apart from the female. Rather, he lumps then into "man" in his anaphonic anchorage of the creation. Subsequently, he chooses "his", "him" and "everyone" when he means to track the singular "man", and "some" when he intends to state the plural, whose synonym is "some people" if enriched (cf Sperber and Wilson 1987; Odebunmi 2005). It should be rewarding to attempt a consideration of a possible gender influence on the gender – neutral and gender- balanced items. The tables below show the distributions on gender bases.

Table 7: Men and Gender/Balanced Items

Variable	Item	Frequency	Percentage
Men and women Gender: Male	Humankind	02	1.10
	The people	08	4.42
	Humanity	09	4.97
	Male and female	11	6.08
	Human being	30	16.57
	All people	05	2.76
	Humans	63	34.81
	Everyone/anyone his/her, him/her	25	13.81
	Us	08	4.42
	We	20	11.05
	Total	181	100

Table 8: Women and Gender-Neutral/Balanced Items

Variable	Item	Frequency	Percentage
Men and women	Humankind	00	00
	The people	00	00
	Humanity	00	00
	Male and female	00	00
	Human being	04	26.67
	All people	01	06.67
	Humans	05	33.33
	Everyone/anyone his/her, him/her	03	20.00
	Us	00	00
	We	02	13.33
	Total	15	100

While Table 7 shows that all the gender items are engaged by men albeit in different, sometimes, low degrees, only 5 out of the ten items are used by women. The two genders have as their highest occurrences "humans", the reason for which can be got from the earlier explanation regarding the topic of the essay and the factor of default plural. The same applies to "human being" which men apply at 16.57% and women at 26.67%. There is also some degree of correlation between the men's engagement of "everyone…" and "we", both of which apply to humanity in general. There is however a clear difference in the genders' realisation of "all people" which is ranked fifth in the women category, and ranked ninth in the men category.

It is difficult to read a strictly sexist meaning into the realisations of the items, merely based on the figures and the varying occurrences. This is because all the items are engaged by the two groups to describe general human experiences, and sometimes to find alternative plural forms for the generic "man" (by both genders) and "mankind" (by the male gender only). However, a scrutiny of contextual uses by the groups brings out some ideological indices which point to their various perspectives of the religious institution and gender roles in the institution. This issue will be handled with respect to "human", "human being" and "everyone…." First, it is observed that despite the neutral nature of "humans", many of the female subjects still assign patriarchal anaphors to it. An example is shown below:

Ex.10
Moreso, despite all the love
that God showed to ***human,*** [sic]
he still went ahead and
disobeyed him.

The 'he' here used by a female subject tracking "human" [s] is ordinarily unacceptable. But Beyond the grammar of the construction, the ideology of institutionalised subservience leaks, which fights against the tenets of feminist theology. On the other hand, the male subjects are more consistent in their use of pronouns tracking "humans", as there is hardly any such use as "she" to refer to "human" in any context. Generally, these subjects track the item with the plural pronoun "they/their", or repeat the item as many times as they need to refer to it. Where an error occurs in terms of number, male subjects prefer "he/him" to track "human". Some of these points are demonstrated below:

> Ex.11
> [God] chose **human** [sic] to rule
> over everything created. As if
> that is not enough, God
> created **human.** He created **him**
> in his own image.

In Ex. 11, "human" is repeated in sentence 2. The error of number in "human[s]" notwithstanding, "him" is used by the male subject to track "human".

The patriarchal attachment to "human" is also evident in "human being" in the essays written by the women. In cases where "human beings" is used, the female subjects select 'they' or "their" as may be applicable but where the error form "human being" is used, the female subject largely opts for the patriarchal pronoun "he" and its variants. An example follows:

> Ex.12
> God loves human being [sic], he
> also needs to love God in
> return.

Evident here is the default "he" which has been imposed by the religious institution and culture as stated earlier. However, on the part of men, the same pattern of use as of "human" is observed.

"Everyone", "anyone", "whosever" (etc), "his/her', and 'him/her' are used in two different ways. It is here that the women are seen to express some degree of assertiveness. In cases where female subjects use any of the partitive pronouns, "his/her" or "him/her" usually follows, as appropriate. The example below explains this:

> Ex.13:
> ...**anybody** who accepts this
> Son as **his** or **her** personal

> Lord and Saviour would be free
> from the punishment of sin

In Ex.13, "his/her" is selected to track the presenting "anybody" by a female subject. This is common in cases where gender-balanced items occur. One could say that the female subjects are free with "his/her" because it also includes men, itself considered a safe way to "play gender" in a highly genderised institution like the Christian religion and a culture like the Yoruba society.

The trend among the men, sometimes, glides with that of the women perhaps largely because it also balances the equation and because it is supported by the English grammar. However, the grammar notwithstanding, some female subjects impose the patriarchal personal pronoun on the partititive or other related items. The following example explains this point:

> Ex.14:
> ...*whoever* knows *himself*
> as a sinner and then confesses and
> repents, He is merciful and faithful
> to forgive *him*

"Him" in Ex. 14 tracks "whoever" in the first part of the extract. Barring grammatical considerations, "himself" and "him" introduce the patriarchal order into the discourse, and emphasise the norm in the main theological context.

Implications of Findings and Conclusion

I have, in the foregoing, discussed, with respect to religious discourse in Nigeria, two terms: patriarchal and gender-neutral/balanced terms. The patriarchal terms bifurcate into terms for God and terms for humans. Both genders opt for patriarchal terms to refer to God and humans. Functional variation, however attends the items used for humans as, while men employ the items subjectively to assert gender superiority, women use them objectively to submit to male dominance.

Both nominal and pronominal items, which are gender-neutral/balanced are used by the genders: 10 by men and 5 by women. Men either draw on the tokens exclusively to subsume women or inclusively to cover both men and women. Women on their part engage the items inclusively by involving both genders and submissively by presuming presenting neutral tokens with patriarchal items.

In the long run, the picture painted by the findings is posed against the situation in the Western world where feminist theology and its tenets have wielded so much in influence. This immediately invites cultural difference as the culprit. For, while many Nigerian cultures are collectivistic in nature, many Western ones are individualistic. Also, while submission to the patriarchal order is fed into the socialisation process of a typical Yoruba (sometimes Nigerian and African) woman, the situation varies in the West. The Christian religious institution, itself a patriarchal religion hosted by cultures which are themselves patriarchy-compliant, could do no less than encourage dominance of the female gender by the male. Hence, it is difficult for the linguistic and theological revolutions in the address system and conception of roles to be allowed good roots in the Nigerian religious soil.

Some studies on gender-neutral usage in the non-religious context have shown some level of awareness of Nigerians with respect to non-genderised terms and expressions. Yusuf and Olateju (2004) have, for example, examined the use of "singular they" among teachers. Lamidi (2009) has studied how academics in a South- western Nigerian University have conceived, applied and accepted gender-neutral pronouns. These studies do not strictly consider gender distinction, yet each has established some level of gender-neutral compliance in English usage by the population. This makes the studies different from the present one and, at the same time, establishes the distinction between secular discourse and religious discourse.

The point is that the English language usage in the religious context in Nigeria complies with the principles of dominance. It is, therefore, necessary for further studies to compare English usage in the religious institution in Nigeria with English usage in other institutions such as medical, academic or commercial. It will also be interesting to compare, perhaps using the same type of population, religious discourse in Nigeria (or Africa) with religious discourse in the West where feminist theology has deep roots.

References

Adams, Jimi. 2007. "Organizational Opposition to Women in Congregational Leadership". *Gender and Society* 21(1): 80-105.

Adegbite, Wale. 2009. "Language, Gender and Politics: A General Perspective". In Akin Odebunmi, Arua E. Arua and Sailal Arimi (eds) *Language, Gender and Politics: A Festschrift for Yisa Kehinde Yusuf.* Lagos: Centre for Black and African Arts and Civilisation, pp. 9-21.

Avishai, Orit. 2008. "Doing Religion in a Secular World: Women in Conservative Religions and the Question of Agency".*Gender and Society* 22(4): 409-433.

Bing, J. and Bergvall, J. 1996. "The Question of Questions: Beyond Binary Thinking". In Bergvall, V, Bing, J. and Freed, A (eds) *Rethinking Language and Gender Research: Theory and Practice.* London: Longman, pp.1-30.

Cameron, Deborah. 1998. *The Feminist Critique of Language: A Reader* (2nd edition) London: Routledge

Causey, Sandra. 2009. "Race, Gender and Religion: Shakespeare in Ania Loomba's Othello and the Racial Question". http://shakespearetragedies. suite 101.com/article.cfm/race_gender_and_religion_in_othello. Accessed September 17, 2009.

Cline, Austin. 2009. "Feminist Theology of Liberation: Fighting Patriarchal Assumptions and Attitudes Towards Women". About.com. Accessed September 12, 2009.

Coates, J. and Cameron, D (eds). 1988. *Women in their Speech Communities.* London: Longman.

Corbett, G.G. 1991. *Gender.* Cambridge: Cambridge University Press.

Encyclopedia of Science and Religion. 2009. "Feminist Theology". eNotes.com. Accessed September 14, 2009.

Fairclough, Norman. 2001. *Language and Power* (second edition). England: Pearson Educational Limited.

Gallagher, Sally and Smith, Christian. 1999. "Symbolic Traditionalism and Pragmatic Egalitarianism" .*Gender and Society* 13(2): 211-233.

Gallagher, Sally. 2004. "Where are the Antifeminist Evangelicals ? Evangelical Identity, Subcultural Location, and Attitudes Toward Feminists". *Gender and Society.* 18(4): 451-472

Grohmann, Marianne. 2009. "Feminist Theology and Jewish Christian Dialogue". International Council of Christians and Jews. Accessed September 14, 2009.

Holmes, J. 1993. *An Introduction to Sociolinguistics.* London, Longman.

Huston, Alaine. 2001. "Women, Men and Patriarchal Bargaining in an Islamic Sufi Order: The Tijamiyya in Kano, Nigeria, 1937 to the present". *Gender and Society* 15(5): 734-753

Johnson, S. and Meinhof, U. (eds) *Language and Masculinity.* Oxford: Blackwell.

Lakoff, Robin. 1975. *Language and Women's Place.* New York: Harper and Row.

Lamidi, Tayo. 2009. "Gender-Neutral Pronoun Usage Among Selected Second Language Users of English in Nigeria". In Akin Odebunmi, Arua E. Arua and Sailal Arimi (eds) *Language, Gender and Politics: A Festschrift for Yisa Kehinde Yusuf.* Lagos Centre for Black and African Arts and Civilisation, Pp. 191-211.

Martin, J. and Rose, D. 2003. *Working with Discourse.* London and New York: Continuum.

Mills, Sara. 2003. *Gender and Politeness.* Cambridge: Cambridge University Press.

Odebunmi, Akin. 2005. "Co-operation in Doctor-patient Conversational Interactions in Southwestern Nigerian Hospitals". In Olateju, Moji and Oyeleye, Lekan (eds) *Perspectives on Language and Literature.* Ile – Ife: Obafemi Awolow Univeristy Press, Pp. 238-252.

Odebunmi, Akin. 2008. "Tracking and Ideology in Politcal News Reporting". *Political Linguistics.* 26(3): 80-87

Queen, R. 1997. "I Don't speak spritch: Loacting Lesbian Language". In Livia, A and Hall, K (eds) *Queerly Phrased: Language, Gender and Sexuality.* London: Routledge, Pp. 233-242.

Read Jen'nan and Bartkwoskii, John. 2000. "To veil or not to veil? A Case Study of Identity Negotiation Among Muslim Women in Austin, Texas". *Gender and Society* 14(3): 395-417.

Spender, D. 1980. *Man Made Language.* London: Routledge.

Sperber, D. and Wilson, D. 1986. *Relevance*. Cambridge: Harvard University Press.

Tannen, D. 1991. *You Just Don't Understand: Women and Men in Conversation*. London: Virago.

Troemel-Ploetz, S. 1998. "Selling the Apolitical". In Coates J(ed) *Language and Gender: A Reader*. Oxford: Blackwell, pp. 446-458.

Witting, M. 1992. *The Straight Mind and Other Essays*. Hemel Hempstead: Harvester.

Wodak, Ruth. 1996. *Disorders and Discourse*. London and New York: Longman.

Wodak, Ruth. 2007. "Pragmatics and Critical Discourse Analysis: A Cross-Disciplinary Inquiry". *Pragmatics and Cognition* 15(1): 203-225.

Wolkomier, Michelle. 2004. "Giving it up to God: Negotiating Femininity in Support Groups for Wives of Ex-gay Christian Men". *Gender and Society* 18(6): 732-755.

Yusuf, Yisa Kehinde and Olateju, Moji 2004. "Singular They and the Nigerian Examines of School Certificate English". In Owolabi, Kola and Dasylua, Ademola (eds) *Forms and Functions of English and Indigenous Languages in Nigeria: A Festschrift in Honour of Ayo Banjo*. Ibadan: Group Publishers, pp. 148-178.

Yusuf, Yisa Kehinde. 1988. "A Critique of the Linguistic Argument for the Possibility of Dexesing Though by Degendering English". *Ife Studies in English Language* 2(1):87-92

Yusuf, Yisa Kehinde. 1993. "The Diffusion of the Male-favoured Praising, Persuasion and Consolation in Yoruba and Sexist Naming in English". *Research in Yoruba Language and Literature*. 4:1001-4

Yusuf, Yisa Kehinde. 1997: (a) "Yoruba Proverbial Insights into Female Sexuality and Genital Mutilation". *Ela: Journal of Africa Studies*. 182: 118-129.

Yusuf, Yisa Kehinde. 1997: (b) "'To Propose is Human" Eliminating sexist language from English proverbs". *Studia Anglica Posnaniensia*. 32:169-178.

www.ingramcontent.com/pod-product-compliance
Lightning Source LLC
Chambersburg PA
CBHW021945290426
44108CB00012B/970